Samuel Edward Dawson

The Voyages of the Cabots in 1497 and 1498

With an Attempt to Determine their Landfall and...

Samuel Edward Dawson

The Voyages of the Cabots in 1497 and 1498
With an Attempt to Determine their Landfall and...

ISBN/EAN: 9783744722506

Printed in Europe, USA, Canada, Australia, Japan

Cover: Foto ©Andreas Hilbeck / pixelio.de

More available books at **www.hansebooks.com**

THE

VOYAGES OF THE CABOTS

IN 1497 AND 1498.

WITH AN ATTEMPT TO DETERMINE THEIR LANDFALL AND TO

IDENTIFY THEIR ISLAND OF ST. JOHN.

.

By SAMUEL EDWARD DAWSON, Lit. D.

FROM THE

TRANSACTIONS OF THE ROYAL SOCIETY OF CANADA,

VOLUME XII, SECTION II, 1894.

MONTREAL

W. FOSTER BROWN & CO., PUBLISHERS.

1894.   .

II.—*The Voyages of the Cabots in 1497 and 1498; with an attempt to determine their landfall and to identify their island of St. John.*

By SAMUEL EDWARD DAWSON, Lit.D.

(Presented May 22, 1894.)

1.—INTRODUCTION.

his continent has been the subject of so much
two Cabots. Their personal character, their
y made and the extent and direction of their
\sputed over. The share, moreover, of each in
ery battleground for historians. Some learned
, others would put him aside and award all the
es even of the voyages are disputed; and very
) not hesitate to declare that the voyages are
ie whole question a mystification.
of the Cabots have always rested the original
pon this continent. In the published annals of
of them exist; nor was there for sixty years in
ichievements. The English claims rest almost
solely upon second hand evidence from Spanish and Italian authors, upon contemporary reports of Spanish and Italian envoys at the English court, upon records of the two letters patent issued, and upon two or three entries lately discovered in the accounts of disbursements from the privy purse of king Henry VII. These are our title-deeds to this continent. The evidence is doubtless conclusive, but the whole subject of western discovery was undervalued and neglected by England for so long a period that it is no wonder if Portuguese savants deny the reality of those voyages, seeing that their nation has been supplanted by a race which can show so little original evidence of its claims.

It may appear presumptuous for a Canadian, far away from the great libraries of the world, to venture into paths trodden by so many able and learned historians; but the labours of Humboldt and Kunstmann, and Kohl, and Kretschmer, and Deane, and Harrisse, and Biddle, and Winsor have brought into accessible shape all the data now extant for forming a judgment, and Canadians can bring to the discussion the advantage of an intimate local knowledge which these learned men could not possess. For that part of continental America first trodden by Europeans is Canadian land, and to Canadians nothing concerning John Cabot can be considered foreign. When Ferland or Bourinot, or Pope, or Patterson, or Laverdière, or Ganong write upon this subject they are writing of seas and coasts familiar

II.—*The Voyages of the Cabots in 1497 and 1498 ; with an attempt to determine their landfall and to identify their island of St. John.*

By Samuel Edward Dawson, Lit.D.

(Presented May 22, 1894.)

1.—Introduction.

Probably no question in the history of this continent has been the subject of so much discussion as the lives and voyages of the two Cabots. Their personal character, their nationality, the number of the voyages they made and the extent and direction of their discoveries have been, and still are, keenly disputed over. The share, moreover, of each in the credit due for the discoveries made is a very battleground for historians. Some learned writers attribute everything to John Cabot, others would put him aside and award all the credit to his second son, Sebastian. The dates even of the voyages are disputed ; and very learned professors of history in Portugal do not hesitate to declare that the voyages are apocryphal, the discoveries pretended, and the whole question a mystification.

Nevertheless solely upon the discoveries of the Cabots have always rested the original claims of the English race to a foothold upon this continent. In the published annals of England, however, no contemporary records of them exist ; nor was there for sixty years in English literature any recognition of their achievements. The English claims rest almost solely upon second hand evidence from Spanish and Italian authors, upon contemporary reports of Spanish and Italian envoys at the English court, upon records of the two letters patent issued, and upon two or three entries lately discovered in the accounts of disbursements from the privy purse of king Henry VII. These are our title-deeds to this continent. The evidence is doubtless conclusive, but the whole subject of western discovery was undervalued and neglected by England for so long a period that it is no wonder if Portuguese savants deny the reality of those voyages, seeing that their nation has been supplanted by a race which can show so little original evidence of its claims.

It may appear presumptuous for a Canadian, far away from the great libraries of the world, to venture into paths trodden by so many able and learned historians ; but the labours of Humboldt and Kunstmann, and Kohl, and Kretschmer, and Deane, and Harrisse, and Biddle, and Winsor have brought into accessible shape all the data now extant for forming a judgment, and Canadians can bring to the discussion the advantage of an intimate local knowledge which these learned men could not possess. For that part of continental America first trodden by Europeans is Canadian land, and to Canadians nothing concerning John Cabot can be considered foreign. When Ferland or Bourinot, or Pope, or Patterson, or Laverdière, or Ganong write upon this subject they are writing of seas and coasts familiar to them from boyhood under every aspect of sunshine and storm. This is a most important auxiliary to book-knowledge and prevents many misconceptions. One instance may suffice —Mr. Harrisse is arguing [1] for a theory that the Portuguese Fagundes, possessed, in 1521, an intimate knowledge of the gulf of St. Lawrence, and he seizes upon the name Aguada bay. This he translates by "Watering bay" from the "place where vessels went to fill their casks with fresh water at the entrance of the St. Lawrence river." Having made this assumption, probably from a supposed analogy with the Amazon which is reported to freshen the water out of sight of land, he naturally concludes that when Fagundes went up the gulf for fresh water he would have seen Prince Edward island, the Magdalens, and Anticosti. Probably he would; but then before he could fill his casks he must have gone 550 miles from the strait of Canso, because the St. Lawrence water is not fresh below Crane island 34 miles from Quebec. To a Canadian the absurdity of vessels coming up from the maritime provinces to Quebec for fresh water is palpable; but, from want of that local knowledge, the immense research of Mr. Harrisse is led into a false path. Canadians should not quietly resign Cabot into other hands, for he is more to them than Columbus is to the people of the United States. Cabot sailed in the service of the British crown and he landed on territory which still owns allegiance to the queen of England. . And then our own gulf —all our own—we, who know it in all its moods—who have seen the gloomy forest steeps of Cape North and the inaccessible cliffs of the Bird Rocks lit by the sun or when the ice was grinding at their bases and the fog sullenly lifting from their summits—we who know its waters when black with storm or rippling in inconstant beauty under the clear blue of our northern summer—we have a commentary on the books and charts which all the learning of a Humboldt or the minute research of a Harrisse can never supply.

It is not my intention to wander over all the debatable ground of the Cabot voyages, where every circumstance bristles with conflicting theories. The original authorities are few and scanty, but mountains of hypotheses have been built upon them, and, too often, the suppositions of one writer have been the facts of a succeeding one. Step by step the learned students before alluded to have established certain propositions which appear to me to be true and which I shall accept without further discussion. Among these I count the following : [2]

1.—That John Cabot was a Venetian, of Genoese birth, naturalized at Venice on March 28th, 1476, after the customary fifteen years of residence; and that he subsequently settled in England with all his family.

2.—That Sebastian, his second son, was born in Venice and when very young was taken by his father to England with the rest of the family.

3.—That on petition of John Cabot and his three sons, Lewis, Sebastian and Sancio, letters patent of king Henry VII. were issued, under date March 5, 1496, empowering them, at their own expense, to discover and take possession for England of new lands not before found by any Christian nation.

4.—That John Cabot, accompanied perhaps by his son Sebastian, sailed from Bristol early in May, 1497. He discovered and landed upon some part of America between Cape Cod, in Massachusetts, and Cape Chidley, in Labrador; that he returned to Bristol before the end of July of the same year; that whatever might have been the number of vessels which started, the discovery was made by John Cabot's own vessel, the "Matthew of Bristol," with a crew of eighteen men.

5.—That thereupon, and in consideration of this discovery made by John Cabot, king Henry VII. granted new letters patent, drawn solely to John Cabot, authorizing a second expedition on a more extended scale and with fuller royal authority, which letters patent were dated February 3rd, 1498. That this expedition sailed in the spring of 1498, and had not returned in October. It consisted of several ships and about three hundred men. That John and Sebastian Cabot sailed on this voyage. When it returned is not known. From the time of sailing of this expedition John Cabot vanishes into the unknowable, and from thenceforth Sebastian alone appears in the historic record.

These points are now fully supported by satisfactory evidence, mostly documentary and contemporary. As for John Cabot, Sebastian said he died, which is one of the few undisputed facts in the discussion; but if Sebastian is correctly reported in Ramusio[3] to have said that he died at the time when the news of Columbus's discoveries reached England, then Sebastian Cabot told an untruth, because the letters patent of 1498 were addressed to John Cabot alone. The son had a gift of reticence concerning others, including his father and brothers, which in these latter days has been the cause of much wearisome research to scholars. To avoid further discussion of the preceding points is, however, a great gain. The aim of the present paper is mainly to ascertain the landfall of John Cabot in 1497, and, incidentally, to identify the island of St. John, discovered on the same day, viz., on St. John the Baptist's day. In attempting this, other points of interest in the historical geography of the gulf of St. Lawrence will necessarily arise.

II. THEORIES OF THE LANDFALL.

From among the numerous opinions concerning the landfall of John Cabot three theories emerge which may be seriously entertained, all three being supported by evidence of much weight.

    1st. That it was in Newfoundland.[4]
    2nd. That it was on the Labrador coast.[5]
    3rd. That it was on the island of Cape Breton.[6]

Until a comparatively recent period it was universally held by English writers that Newfoundland was the part of North America first seen by Cabot. The name New-foundland lends itself to this view; for, in the letters patent of 1498, the expression, "Londe and iles of late founde," and the wording of the award recorded in the king's privy purse accounts, August 10, 1497, "To hym that founde the new ile £10," seem naturally to suggest the island of Newfoundland of our day; and this impression is strengthened by reading the old authors, who spell it, as Richard Whitbourne in 1588, New-found-land,[7] in three words with connecting hyphens, and often with the definite article, "The Newe-found-land." A cursory reading of the whole literature of American discovery before 1831 would suggest that idea, and some writers of the present day still maintain it. Authors of other nationalities have, however, always disputed it, and have pushed the English discoveries far north, to Labrador and even to Greenland. Champlain,[8] who read and studied everything relating to his profession, concedes to the English the coast of Labrador north of 56° and the regions about Davis straits; and the maps, which for a long period, with a few notable exceptions, were made only by Spaniards, Portuguese and Italians, bear out Champlain's remonstrances. It seems, moreover, on a cursory consideration of the maps, probable that a vessel on a westerly course passing south of Ireland should strike somewhere on the coast of Newfoundland about Cape Bonavista, and Cabot being an Italian, that very place suggests itself by its name as his probable landfall. The English, who for the most part have had their greatness thrust upon them by circumstances, neglected Cabot's discoveries for fifty years and during that time the French and Portuguese took possession of the whole region and named all the coasts; then when the troubled reign of Henry VIII. was over, the English people began to wake up and in fact re-discovered Cabot and his voyages. A careful study however of the subject will be likely to lead to the rejection of the Newfoundland landfall—plausible as it may at first sight appear.

In the year 1831 Richard Biddle, a lawyer of Pittsburg in Pennsylvania, published a memoir of Sebastian Cabot which led the way to an almost universal change of opinion. He advanced the theory that Labrador was the Cabot landfall in 1497. His book is one of great research and, though confused in its arrangement, is written with much vigour and ability. But Biddle lost the historian in the advocate. His book is a passionate brief for Sebastian Cabot; for he strangely conceives the son to have been wronged by the ascription to John Cabot of any portion of the merit of the discovery of America. Not only would he suppress the elder Cabot, but he covers the well-meaning Hakluyt with opprobrium and undermines his character by insinuations, much as a criminal lawyer might be supposed to do to an adverse witness in a jury trial. Valuable as the work is there is a singular heat prevading it, fatal to the true historic spirit. Hakluyt is the pioneer of the literature of English discovery and adventure—at once the recorder and inspirer of noble effort. He is more than a translator; he spared no pains nor expense to obtain from the lips of seamen their own versions of their voyages, and, if discrepancies are met with in a collection so voluminous, it is not surprising and need not be ascribed to a set purpose; for Hakluyt's sole object in life seems to have been to record all he knew or could ascertain of the maritime achievements of the age.

Biddle's book marks an epoch in the controversy. In truth he seems to be the first who gave minute study to the original authorities and broke away from the tradition of Newfoundland. He fixed the landfall on the coast of Labrador and Humboldt and Kohl added the weight of their great learning to his theory. Harrisse, who in his John and Sebastian Cabot had written in favour of Cape Breton has, in his latest book, "The Discovery of America," gone back to Labrador as his faith in the celebrated map of 1544 gradually waned-and his esteem for the character of Sebastian Cabot faded away. Such changes of view, not only in this but in other matters, render Mr. Harrisse's books somewhat confusing, although the student of American history can never be sufficiently thankful for his untiring research.

The discovery in Germany by Von Martius in 1843 of an engraved *mappemonde* bearing date of 1544 and purporting to be issued under the authority of Sebastian Cabot, soon caused a general current of opinion in favour of a landfall in Cape Breton. The map is unique and is now in the National Library at Paris. It bears no name of publisher nor place of publication. Around it for forty years controversy has waxed warm. Kohl does not accept the map as authentic. D'Avezac,[*] on the contrary, gives it full credence. The tide of opinion has set of late in favour of it and in consequence in favour of the Cape Breton landfall because it bears, plainly inscribed upon that island, the words *prima tierra vista*, and the legends which are around the map identify beyond question that as the landfall of the first voyage. Dr. Deane, in "Winsor's Narrative and Critical History," supports this view. Markham in his introduction to the volume of the Hakluyt Society for 1893 also accepts it and our own honorary secretary in his learned and exhaustive monograph on Cape Breton [10] inclines to the same theory.

I do not propose, in this portion of my paper, to discuss the difficult problems of this map. For many years, under the influence of current traditions and cursory reading, I believed the landfall of John Cabot to have been in Newfoundland; but a closer study of the original authorities has led me to concur in the view which places it somewhere on the island of Cape Breton, and this view I shall endeavour, in the first instance, to establish without recourse to the disputed map of 1544. That map has, I conceive, introduced into current belief a very serious error by putting forth, as is supposed, Prince Edward Island as the island of St. John of Cabot's first voyage. This error is gaining ground every day as it is passing into all our histories [11] and guide books. In the course of this paper I shall endeavour to explain the reasons which move me to dissent from it. And while it seems clear that the landfall of 1497 was on the island of Cape Breton, I shall endeavour to show that it was not at Cape North, but rather at the easternmost point of the island at or near Cape Breton itself. In short it will, I think, appear that the more the attention is fixed upon Sebastian Cabot the more we shall think of Labrador; but when John Cabot alone is considered we shall incline to believe that the landfall was at Cape Breton.

III. The First and Second Voyages contrasted, 1497 and 1498.

At the very threshold of an inquiry into the *prima tierra vista*, or landfall of 1497, it is before all things necessary to distinguish sharply, in every recorded detail, between the first and second voyages. I venture to think that, if this had always been done, much confusion and controversy would have been avoided. It was not done by the older writers, and the writers of later years have followed them without sufficiently observing that the authorities they were building upon were referring almost solely to the second voyage. Even when some occasional detail of the first voyage was introduced the circumstances of the second voyage were interwoven and became dominant in the narrative, so that the impression of one voyage only remains upon the mind. We must therefore always remember the antithesis which exists between them. Thus—the first voyage was made in one small vessel with a crew of eighteen men [12]—the second with five ships and three hundred men.[13] The first voyage was undertaken with John Cabot's own resources—the second with the royal authority to take six ships and their outfit on the same conditions as if for the king's service. [14] The first voyage was a private venture—the second an official expedition. [14] The first voyage extended over three months and was provisioned for that period only, [15] the second was victualled for twelve months [16] and extended over six months at least; for how much longer is not known. The course of the first voyage was south of Ireland, then for a while north and afterwards west, with the pole star [17] on the right hand. The course of the second, until land was seen, was north,[18] into northern seas, towards the north pole, in the direction of Iceland,[19] to the cape of Labrador, at 58° north latitude. On the first voyage no ice was reported—on the second the leading features were bergs [20] and floes of ice and long days of Arctic summer. On the first voyage Cabot saw no man [21]—on the second he found people clothed with "beastes skynnes." [21] During the whole of the first voyage John Cabot was the commander [22]—on the second voyage he sailed in command, [21] but who brought the expedition home and when it returned are not recorded. It is not known how or when John Cabot died and, although the letters patent for the second voyage were addressed to him alone, his son Sebastian during forty-five years took the whole credit in every subsequent mention of the discovery of America without any allusion to his father. This antithesis may throw light upon the suppression of his father's name in all the statements attributed to or made by Sebastian Cabot. He may always have had the second voyage in his mind. His father may have died on the voyage. He was marvellously reticent about his father. The only mention which occurs is on the map seen by Hakluyt and on the map of 1544 supposed, somewhat rashly, to be a transcript of it. There the discovery is attributed to John Cabot and to Sebastian his son and that has reference to the first voyage. [25]

From these considerations it would appear that those who place the landfall at Labrador are right; but it is the landfall of the second voyage—the voyage Sebastian was always talking about—not the landfall of John Cabot in 1497. For Sebastian manifested no concern for any person's reputation but his own. He never once alluded to his two brothers who were associated in the first patent and the preceding slight notice of his father is all that can be traced to him, although contemporary records of unquestionable authority indicate John Cabot as the moving spirit and do not mention the son.

Since that period the point of interest has changed. Wile we are chiefly exercised about the voyage of 1497, in Cabot's day that of 1498 was of paramount importance; for it alone had political significance. We approach the question as antiquarians; but then it was a question in practical politics. The public and official voyage in the usage of that time gave a prescriptive right to the lands discovered. So little had the first voyage of a formal possession for England alone that Cabot planted the banner of St. Mark [21] beside that of St. George and any public right arising from that ceremony might accrue to Venice as well as to England. The existence of land across the ocean within easy distance having thus been demonstrated the cautious and politic Henry was induced to give the fullest national sanction to the second voyage. These new lands were supposed to be part of eastern Asia; and there everything was possible. Upon Toscanelli's map and Behaim's globe the region of Cathay and the great cities of Quinsay and Cambaluc lay in the same latitudes as the new-found-land; therefore the mere touching at a point on the coast and immediate return was of little importance compared with the range of the second voyage. Then again, to do Sebastian Cabot justice, he seems, like Juan de la Cosa, very soon to have apprehended the fact that those western lands were a barrier to Cathay, and that a passage would have to be found through or around them. Columbus died without admitting that fact, but it is remarkable that the coast line of so many of the very earliest charts is continuous. Hence, in all his reported conversations, Sebastian Cabot dwelt upon a passage by the north, on a great circle, to Cathay. We on the contrary care for none of these things. The northwest passage to Cathay and the nationality of America have been settled in the lapse of time beyond all cavil, and what we are concerned to solve is the historical problem: who first discovered the mainland of America? For that reason John Cabot and his little vessel the "Matthew of Bristol" [27] have to us a paramount interest.

In this portion of my paper, then, Peter Martyr, Gomara, Ramusio and Hakluyt are of minor importance. I am to concern myself first with those Spanish and Italian envoys whose letters and despatches from England in that same year are almost the only contemporary evidence we possess of John Cabot's achievement. As these were all written before the return of the second expedition, in studying them we are sure of having the only extant information concerning the first voyage absolutely free from any intermixture with the details of the second.

IV. Variation of the Compass in 1497.

Thus far I have been considering the two Cabot voyages together, in their contrasts ; and now I shall endeavour to detach them the one from the other in all the details which remain of record ; but, before doing so, some attention must be devoted to the mariner's compass as then in use, for it was then, as now, the reliance of all sailors in unknown seas. I should never have attempted even to refer to so difficult a question, had it not been for the reports of the United States Coast and Geodetic Survey for 1880 and 1888 which contain papers by Mr. Chas. A. Schott and Capt. Fox. By the aid of those very valuable papers it became possible to form an intelligent opinion as to what can and what cannot be known about the variation of the compass in the North Atlantic in 1497.

The mariner's compass had been in use in Europe since the middle of the 12th century. At the time of Columbus and Cabot it was, in all essential parts, like that now in use. The card was divided into 32 points of 11¼ degrees each. It had been observed that the needle did not point exactly to the pole star ; but the variation was then very slight ; in southern and western Europe only about $5°$; or less than half a point. What variation there was was to the east of north and it was supposed to be constant ; hence, when, on his first voyage to America in 1492, Columbus noticed that the needle crossed over to the west, one-half point in the evening and another half point the next morning, he was very much astonished ; and when, four days later, on September 17th, his pilots noticed it their hearts sank with apprehension at entering a world of waters where even the magnetic needle might become a treacherous guide. This observation by Columbus we may well understand was a very serious and solemn one ; and it fixes beyond all doubt the meridian of no variation at a point west of the Azores, in latitude 28° N. and longitude about 28° W. At the present time the variation at the point of first notice is 25 degrees or nearly double that observed by Columbus and it therefore follows that all over the North Atlantic, the compass marked in 1497 a much less westerly variation than it does now. From this first observation, and from the long series of observations since made with increasing accuracy and frequency, it has been ascertained that, subject to local conditions, there is a slow swing of the magnetic meridian from east to west and vice versa extending over centuries of time. This has been called the secular variation of the compass. Its cause is not known, its laws are not fully ascertained, but it is a fertile source of confusion among students who plot out early voyages in northern seas solely with the aid of modern maps.

While Columbus, sailing on the latitude of 28', was proceeding always in the direction where the variation was slight, Cabot's course in the north was in a region of greater variation ; being so much the nearer to the magnetic pole. For Columbus was sailing on a west course which he scarcely deviated from, because although on the last three days of the voyage he steered S. W., and W. S. W., there were previous days when he made a little northing. Nevertheless when he reached land the admiral had dropped 240 miles to the south of Gomara his point of departure.

If the laws of the secular variation of the compass were known it would be easy to calculate the variation at any given period ; but they are not known, and so we are driven to argue empirically from the observations recorded, and these do not commence on our coast until the time of Champlain. But that is two hundred and fifty years nearer to Cabot's time and, as the secular magnetic swing is very slow, his observations, of which a few are recorded, are of great importance. These all confirm the opinion stated that the variation was considerably less then than now. The variation at Sydney, Cape Breton, is at present 25° W., at Cape Race it is 30° W. and at Halifax it stands at 25° ; the extreme westerly limit has been reached this year.

The officers of the Geodetic Survey think that Champlain's observations are from 1° to 3° out, and moreover it is hard to see how the progression of westerly variation could increase in a southwest direction. It is contrary to the magnetic curves of the present time that the variation should be 14° 50' at Cape Breton ; 16° 15' at La Hève near Halifax ; 17° 8' at Port Royal on the Annapolis Basin; 17° 16' at Petit Passage ; 19° 12' at the Kennebec and 18° 40' at Mallebarre in Massachusetts (Nauset). Still there is a progression in these figures which does not look like careless observation and Champlain (see appendix A) was by no means careless in anything he undertook. That, however, is a question in magnetism which fortunately it is not necessary to discuss. Other observations were made by Hendrick Hudson about the same time which run more in accord with present theories ; and, in the "Arcano del Mare" published at Florence in 1646, a number of observations are recorded which give unquestionable evidence of accuracy ; those taken for Cape Breton, and St. Johns, Newfoundland, agree in assigning to these localities a magnetic variation of 15 degrees west of north. The bearing of these considerations upon the present question is, shortly, this : If Columbus on a direct western course dropped 240 miles from Gomara his point of departure to his landfall in the Antilles in 1492 with a variation of one point west, it is altogether probable that John Cabot with a variation of a point and a half would have dropped, in 1497, 360 miles to the south on his western course across the Atlantic ; and, again, if John Cabot laid his course to the west by compass from latitude 53° north the variation, so much greater than that observed by Columbus, would have carried him clear of Cape Race and to the next probable landfall, Cape Breton. In any case, Labrador as a landfall, is excluded.

V. The First Voyage, 1497.

In the despatch of Pedro de Ayala dated July 25th, 1498, to the court of Spain he asserts that John Cabot had previously been in Seville and in Lisbon trying to obtain assistance for a voyage to the west, and, it would appear, that, failing there, he had gone to Bristol. The people of Bristol, one may gather from the despatch, stimulated by him, had been for seven years sending out vessels to look for the island of Brasil in the western ocean but without success until 1497, when land was found. Of these previous efforts and previous voyages no other traces have been found and the first we hear of John Cabot is in the letters patent of March 5th, 1496, upon the petition of himself and his three sons, Lewis, Sebastian and Sancio, empowering them, at their own expense, to fit out an expedition to discover new lands and take possession thereof for the English crown. The jealousy of the Spanish envoy was awakened before the letters were granted, and a rescript of the Catholic sovereigns to Dr. de Puebla dated March 28th, 1496, instructs him to represent to the king of England that such enterprises could not be undertaken without prejudice to the rights of either Spain or Portugal. Doubtless de Puebla had anticipated his sovereigns' command, for the wording of the letters patent limits the scope of the projected discoveries to the north, the east and the west, without mentioning the south. A year passed before the preparations could be made and, early in May, 1497, Cabot sailed from Bristol, the port prescribed in the patent. That port is in latitude 51° 30′ N., and the objective point of Cabot's voyage was Cathay the capital city of which kingdom was Cambaluc in latitude 51° N., according to Toscanelli's map.[29] Upon that map Columbus had plotted his course only five years before, and he sailed first south to Gomara, in the Azores, in order to get upon the parallel of Cipango his objective point, which he thought he had reached by following that parallel on an undeviating western course. In like manner John Cabot sought Cathay. He could not then have had a thought of a northwest passage for he knew, then, of no barrier. For him, as for Columbus, the western ocean was open to the coast of Asia. Columbus had attained Cipango, on a parallel of latitude ten degrees to the south of Spain. Cabot sailing from a port eleven degrees to the north of Spain would reach the mainland of Asia at Cathay twenty degrees north of Cipango, for Quinsay the southernmost city of that great country was in latitude 45° N., and he would have, moreover, the advantage of sailing on a parallel where the degrees of longitude are much shorter. This could be done without approaching by 20 degrees of latitude the regions claimed by Spain. John Cabot had therefore no object in going north. Why should he be supposed to have wished to go north when his course was open across the western ocean? The only northing he needed was what might be sufficient to keep his true west in sailing on a sphere. He had no occasion to make more. The importance of keeping this objective point in mind cannot be too much insisted upon. What Cipango was to Columbus, Quinsay and Cambaluc [30] were to Cabot. Therefore he sailed south of Ireland which he would not have done had any idea of a northern voyage been in his mind. If Sebastian Cabot had not been so much wrapped up in his own vain glory we might have had a full record of the eventful voyage which revealed to Europe the shores of our Canadian dominion first of all the lands on the continents of the western hemisphere. Fortunately, however, there resided in London at that time a most intelligent Italian, Raimondo di Soncino, envoy of the duke of Milan, Ludovico Sforza, one of those despots of the Renaissance who almost atoned for their treachery and cruelty by their thirst for knowledge and love of arts. Him Soncino kept informed of all matters going on at London and specially concerning matters of cosmography to which the duke was much devoted. From his letters we are enabled to retrace the momentous voyage of the little "Matthew of Bristol" across the western ocean—not the sunny region of steady trade-winds by whose favouring influence Columbus was wafted to his destination, but the boisterous reaches of the northern Atlantic—over that "still vexed sea" which shares with one or two others the reputation of being the most storm tossed region in the world of ocean. Passing Ireland he first shaped his course north, then, turning westwards [31] and having the pole star on his right hand, he wandered for a long time and at length he hit upon land. The letter indicates that after he changed his course his wandering was continuously westwards, in the same general direction, as far as the regions of the Tanais. No certain meaning can be found for the word Tanais; but inasmuch as in those days the Tanais was held to separate Europe from Asia [32] it may be taken as a vague term for Asiatic lands. That the land discovered was supposed to be a part of Asia appears very clearly from the same letters. It was in the territory of the Grand Cam.[31] The land was good and the climate temperate [34] and Cabot intended on his next voyage, after occupying that place, to proceed further westwards until he should arrive at the longitude of Japan which island he evidently thought to be south of his landfall and near the equator.

It should be carefully noted that in all the circumstances on record which are indisputably referable to this first voyage nothing has been said of ice or of any notable extension of daylight. These are the marks of the second voyage; for if anything unusual had existed in the length of the day it would have been at its maximum on midsummer's day, June 24, the day he made land. Nothing is reported in these letters which indicates a high latitude. The shore of Labrador is a waste region of rocks, swamps and mountains. Lieut. Gordon steaming along the coast in the "Alert" passed, on June 30th, 1886, large numbers of small icebergs. He met the field ice on July 2nd at lat. 56° and from lat. 58° to Cape Chidley it was packed tight all along for fifteen miles out to sea. Even inside the straits of Belle-Isle it is so barren and forbidding as to call forth Cartier's oft-cited remark that "it was like the land God gave to Cain." The coast of Labrador is not the place to invite a second voyage, if it be once seen ; but the climate of Cape Breton is very pleasant in early summer and the country is well wooded.

From the contemporary documents relating specially to the first voyage it is beyond question that Cabot saw no human being on the coast though he brought back evidences of their presence at some previous time. It is beyond doubt also on the same authority that the voyage lasted not longer than three months and that provisions gave out so that he had not time to land on the return voyage. It was, in fact, a reconnoitering expedition to prepare the way for a greater effort and establish confidence in the existence of land across the ocean easily reached from England. The distance sailed is given by Soncino at 400 leagues ; but Pasqualigo, writing to Venice, gives it at 700 leagues, equivalent to 2,226 miles, which is very nearly the distance between Bristol and Cape Breton as now estimated.

All these circumstances concerning the first voyage are derived from John Cabot's own reports and are extracted from documents dated previous to the return of the second expedition and therefore are, of necessity, free from admixture with extraneous incidents. I have not referred to the map of 1544 because I propose to consider it by itself. The early historians who are usually cited throw no light upon the first voyage. Peter Martyr in 1516, Gomara in 1542 and Ramusio in 1550 are exclusively concerned with Sebastian Cabot. They know nothing of John Cabot and his voyage and whatever dates they give, the particulars they recite stamp their narratives as relating solely to the second voyage. They, in fact, seem to know only of one. Antonio Galvano an experienced Portuguese sailor and cosmographer writing in 1563, like the others, knows of one voyage only which he fixes in 1496. He interweaves, like them, in his narrative many circumstances of the second voyage, but it is important to note that from some independent source is given the landfall at 45°, the latitude very nearly of Cape Breton on the island of Cape Breton. Another point is also recorded in the letters that, on the return voyage, Cabot passed two islands to the right which the shortness of his provisions prevented him from examining. This note should not be considered identical with the statement recorded by Soncino in his first letter ; for this last writer evidently means to indicate the land which Cabot found and examined—he says that Cabot discovered two large and fertile islands ; but the two islands of Pasqualigo were passed without examination. They were probably the islands of St. Pierre and Miquelon ; but that John Cabot had no idea of a northward voyage at that time in his mind would appear from his intention to sail further to the east on his next voyage until he reached the longitude of Cipango. Moreover, the reward recorded in the king's privy purse accounts "to hym that founde the new ile" and the wording, thrice repeated, of the second letters patent, "the land and isles of late found by the said John" indicate that it was not at that time known whether the mainland of Cathay had been reached or, as in the discoveries of Columbus, islands upon the coast of Asia.

From the preceding narrative, based solely upon documents written within twelve months of the event ; which documents are records of statements taken from the lips of John Cabot, the chief actor, at the very time of his return from the first voyage, it will, I trust, appear that in 1497, at a time of year when the ice was not clear from the coasts of Labrador, he discovered a part of America in a temperate climate ; and that this was done without the name of Sebastian Cabot once coming to the surface, excepting when it appears in the patent of 1496, together with the names of Lewis and Sancio, his brothers. While the circumstances recorded are incompatible with a landfall at Labrador they do not exclude the possibility of a landfall on the eastern coast of Newfoundland, which is so varied in its character as to correspond with almost any conditions likely to be found in a landfall on the American coast ; but inasmuch as, from other reasons, it will, I think, appear that the landfall was at Cape Breton it will be a shorter process to prove by a positive argument where it was than to show by a negative argument where it was not ;—and now, before passing to another branch of my subject it will be proper to notice a theory which Humboldt based on Juan de la Cosa's map that John Cabot passed in between St. Paul's Island and Cape Ray, circumnavigated the gulf of St. Lawrence and returned to England through the straits of Belle-Isle.

Juan de la Cosa's map is a document of such prime importance that it merits separate consideration, but I think, that every one who knows the gulf will share Kohl's astonishment that such a theory should have been held by so eminent a cosmographer. Henry Stevens [35] follows Humboldt, and Dr. Deane doubtingly says, "If the statement about coasting 300 leagues be true he (Cabot) may have made a periplus of the gulf returning by Belle-Isle." The statement is based on a remark made by Pasqualigo, and if there had been time sufficient to sail so far we might be bound to accept it ; but there was not. The log of Columbus [36] sailing in a southern latitude with a steady northeast trade-wind behind him shows an average of 4·4 miles an hour. Cabot sailed in the region of variable winds, therefore the log of John Cabot could not have shown such an average progress, and it did not on the outer voyage for he left Bristol early in May—say the fifth—and saw land on June the 24th, thus making good on a straight course 2,200 miles in 50 days or 44 miles [37] a day, almost two miles an hour. If he delayed only four days to examine the land he had found, and then sailed straight for home he would have made the passage in 30 days, for he certainly arrived at Bristol about the end (say the 28th) of July. That would give a log of 75 miles a day or 3 miles an hour on a straight continuous course. But he did not make such a course, for Juan de la Cosa's map shows that he coasted along and named the south shore of Newfoundland a distance of 300 miles, not leagues. He could not have coasted 935 miles more along the continent of America and have returned home in the time specified, still less was it possible for him to sail around the gulf and return. To Canadians who know the gulf, it is impossible, even if there had been time to do it that he could have sailed round it and not have left some indication of its unique geographical features. He could not have passed the grand estuary of the river opening to the southwest—to the very direction of Cathay—without mentioning it and without returning to it on his second voyage. If he saw, as he must have seen according to that theory, such an avenue opening towards the heart of Asia some tradition of it could not fail to have reached us—some trace of it could not fail to have been recorded on the maps. Of all the theories of John Cabot's voyages that one will appear to a Canadian the most astonishing; as it did to Kohl who had travelled in Canada and knew something of what the name river St. Lawrence implies.

Markham, in his introduction to the Hakluyt Society volume for 1893, makes some excellent observations in relation to the voyage of 1497, and no one could be a better authority than he on such a subject. He thinks that Cabot was compelled by contrary winds to make the northing of the first few days. That north course might be supposed to have brought him to the latitude of 53° or 54°, well north upon the west coast of Ireland, then turning to the west he would have struck for the coast of Cathay. For a good portion of the distance the drift of the ocean is to the northeast as far at least as longitude 40 W. Then he would enter the Arctic or Labrador current which sets south on the banks off Newfoundland at the rate of one mile an hour, but the lee-way assumed by Markham across the ocean would not be always south; for southwest and southerly winds are very common in June, and his lee-way would as often be north as south. The fact, however, which seems to have passed unnoticed is that, in longitude 23° W., he would have passed the point of no variation [x] and have quickly reached a region where the variation of the compass has been shown to be 15° W. On a supposed western course from thence he would be actually steering a point and a half south of west. In those days the incidents of the voyage of Columbus recorded in his journal could not have quickly spread throughout Europe, and Cabot would have had to make his own experiences with the absolutely new phenomenon of magnetic variation. All these circumstances render it in the highest degree probable that he passed Cape Race without seeing it. Then his course would bring him certainly not to Cape North, but to the eastern point of the island, to Cape Breton itself; so that Harrisse in his work on the Cabots was far more nearly right than in his later book on the discovery of America. If Cabot passed Cape Race and the islands of St. Pierre and Miquelon without seeing them he would have been obliged to change his course sharply to the northwest [y] to reach Cape North; and, in fact, the land both of Cape Breton and Newfoundland is so high that, to make Cape North, without first seeing one coast or the other, would require a good deal of nautical skill and a good modern chart; moreover the current out of St. Paul strait sets on the starboard bow of an approaching vessel sometimes as strongly with the prevailing westerly wind as two miles an hour. [40] Cape Breton, as may be seen by Hore's voyage in 1536, was a natural landfall for a vessel missing Cape Race; and so generally recognized as such that in the sailing directions for Sir Humphrey Gilbert's fleet it was laid down as the next rendezvous in case the ships should not meet at Cape Race.

VI. The Second Voyage, 1498.

I might here borrow the quaint phrase of Herodotus and say " now I have done speaking of " John Cabot. He has, beyond doubt, discovered the eastern coast of this our Canada, and he has organized a second expedition, and he has sailed in command. Forthwith, upon such sailing, he vanishes utterly and his second son, Sebastian, both of his brothers having in some unknown way, also vanished, emerges and from henceforth becomes the whole Cabot family. It behooves us, therefore, if we wish to grasp the whole subject, to inquire what manner of man he was.

Sebastian Cabot was born in Venice, and, when still very young, was taken to England with the rest of his family by his father." He was then, however, old enough to have learned the humanities [12] and the properties of the sphere, and to this latter knowledge he became so addicted that he, early in life, formed fixed ideas. He is probably entitled to the merit of having urged the practical application of the truths that the shortest course, from point to point upon the globe, lies upon a great circle; and also that the great circle uniting western Europe with Cathay passes.over the north pole. As a matter of fact the shortest line from England to Japan is by Spitzbergen. We know that as a barren fact; because we know also that the Polar sea is, for practical purposes, impassable; but that Cabot did not know. He could not learn it from the properties of the sphere and he had not learned it in the way of experience. At first it was a very promising route of sailing to India. Robert Thorne, an English merchant living at Seville, points out, in 1527, in representations made privately to the English king, that there is no more reason to suppose the sea to be impassable at the north from cold than there had been to suppose it impassable at the equator from heat. All authorities had concurred in the existence of a southern zone of intolerable heat, and sailors had even brought home reports of having encountered a boiling sea." This had been shown by recent discoveries to be false, and why should not the same authorities be also wrong in their theories of a frozen zone !" So reasoned Robert Thorne who lived at Seville when Sebastian Cabot held there a high position as grand pilot of Spain, and thus insisted Sebastian Cabot from his youth to his extreme old age, and this fixed idea of his became also the fixed idea of the English people; so that they have scarcely recovered from it within our own recollection. Biddle and Nicholls laud him as the "discoverer of great circle sailing and founder of the English mercantile marine." The English marine existed before him, but England owes to him the initiation of the long weary struggle with the frozen ocean which for three centuries has strewn the Arctic wastes with the bodies of her noblest sailors; from Sir Hugh Willoughby who perished with all his gallant crew on the shores of Lapland in 1554, the first fruits of great circle sailing by the north, to Sir John Franklin who perished almost in our own days. Nordenskiold in the Vega in the two years of 1878–9 made the passage Cabot dreamed of in his later years to Japan by way of Spitzbergen, that passage upon which Sir Hugh Willoughby sailed in 1554, and now in this very year Nansen has thrown himself into the ice pack in the hope of drifting across the Polar ocean.

This fixed idea of the younger Cabot pervaded all his life and shows in all his reported conversations. He adhered to it with the pertinacity of a Columbus and, in his later life after his return to England, his efforts which in youth were directed to a northwest passage went out towards a northeast passage to Cathay. John Cabot's genius was more practical, as the second letter of Raimondo di Soncino shows. His intention was to occupy on the second voyage the landfall he had made and then push on to the east (west as we call it now) and south. The diversion of that expedition to the coast of Labrador would indicate that the death of the elder Cabot and the assumption of command by his son occurred early in the voyage. Sebastian Cabot seems to have been, not so much a great sailor, as a great nautical theorizer. Gomara says he discovered nothing for Spain ; and beyond doubt his expedition to La Plata cannot be considered successful ; for it was intended to reach the Moluccas. One fixed idea of his life was the course to Cathay by the north. That idea he monopolized to himself. He overvalued its importance and thought to be the Columbus of a new highway to the east. Hence he may have underrated his father's achievements as he brooded over what he considered to be his own great secret. He theorized on the sphere and he theorized on the variation of the compass and he theorized on a method of finding longitude by the variation of the needle ; so that even Richard Eden, who greatly admired him, wrote as follows : "Sebastian Cabot on his death-bed told me that he had the know-" ledge thereof (longitude by variation) by divine revelation, yet so that he might not teach " any man. But I thinke that the goode olde man in that extreme age somewhat doted " and had not, yet even in the article of death, utterly shaken off all worldlye vaine glorie." These words would seem to contain the solution of most of the mystery of the suppression of John Cabot's name in the narratives of Peter Martyr, Ramusio, Gomara and all the other writers who derived their information from Sebastian Cabot during his long residence in Spain. The remainder of the mystery may be solved in the succeeding portion of this paper.

And now we may pass on to the consideration of the second voyage ; and first among the writers, in order of time as also in order of importance, is Peter Martyr of Anghiera, who published his " Decades of the New World" in 1516. Sebastian Cabot had then been in Spain for four years, high in office and in royal favour. Peter Martyr was his "familiar friend and comrade," and tells the pope, to whom these " Decades" were addressed as letters, that he wrote from information derived from Cabot's own lips. Here, I venture to think, many of the writers on this subject have gone astray ; for the whole question changes. Martyr knows of only one voyage, and that was beyond doubt the voyage of 1498 ; he knows of only one discoverer, and that the man from whose lips he writes the narrative. The landfall is far north, in a region of ice and perpetual daylight. At the very outset the subject is stated to be " those northern seas," and then Peter Martyr goes on to say that Sebastian Cabot furnished two ships at his own charges ; and that, with three hundred men, he sailed towards the north pole, where he saw land ; and that then he was compelled to turn westwards ; and after that he coasted to the south until he reached the latitude of Gibraltar ; and that he was west of the longitude of Cuba. In other words, he struck land far in the north, and from that point he sailed south along the coast as far as Cape Hatteras. That Labrador was the landfall seems clear ; for he met large masses of ice in the month of July. These were not merely the bergs of the western ocean, but masses of field-ice, which compelled him to change his course from north to west, and finally to turn southwards. The same writer states that Cabot himself named a portion of the great land he coasted Baccalaos, because of the quantity of fish, which was so great that they hindered the sailing of his ships, and that these fishes were called baccalaos by the natives. This statement has given rise to much dispute. As to the quantity of fish all succeeding writers concur that it was immense beyond conception ; and probably the swarming of the salmon up the rivers of our Pacific coast may afford a parallel ; but that Cabot did not so name the country is abundantly clear. A very exhaustive note on the word will be found at page 131 of Dr. Bourinot's " Cape Breton." He gives the Micmac name as pegoo, on the authority of Dr. Rand. Richard Brown gives it as pahshoo in his " History of Cape Breton."

Lescarbot gave it in his time as *apegé*. Kohl derives the word, by a parallel evolution, from the Dutch word *kabeljaow*, but, as pointed out by Dr. Bourinot, the word is Basque. It may be called Iberian, for the Basque *bacailaba* became in Spanish *baccalao* and in Portuguese *bacalhas*,[45] and this last name is found on Pedro Reinel's map of 1505. It is not likely that Cabot, in an English ship with an English crew, would have given the country an Iberian name. The probability is that the Portuguese, who flocked upon the coast after the Corte Reals, first gave the name " codfish land " to the country; and Cabot's claim to the name is no more true than his claim to having fitted out the expedition at his own expense. I have read somewhere in the books that Sebastian Cabot was a great sailor and also a great liar, but I think Richard Eden's naive account of his last illness is the best explanation of his very comprehensive claims.

The letter from Cabot which Ramusio[46] quotes had been lost, and we have only Ramusio's recollection of it. That tells us, in general terms, of a voyage to the far north, when a latitude of 67° 30' was attained. In the various accounts which have come down to us as on Cabot's authority different latitudes are given, 56°, 58°, 60°, and here 67° 30". A very high latitude was no doubt attained ; but here, in the recollections of this letter, is a surprising statement that Cabot was on the 11th of June at that latitude, and the sea was then clear[46] and without any manner of impediment, and that he would have sailed straight on to the east at Cathay, but a mutiny of the masters and sailors prevented him, and he had to return. This is not only contradictory to his statements elsewhere, but it is well known that the Labrador coast and Hudson's straits are not accessible, on account of ice, so early in the summer.

It is much to be regretted, for Cabot's own sake as well as for ours, that nothing from his own hand has been preserved either in print or in manuscript ; because his reputation has been entirely at the mercy of the memories of his friends, and, at this distance of time, it is impossible to say whether he was phenomenally addicted to inaccuracy of expression or his friends were phenomenally endowed with treacherous memories. The much quoted conversation in Ramusio is a case in point. Ramusio has recorded, from memory only some years after it occurred, a conversation at the house of his learned friend Frascator. A stranger, whose name is not given, was present among the guests. He was evidently a man of distinction and of learning. The conversation turned upon cosmography, the favourite topic then of cultivated society, and all present were speculating upon the possibility of sailing to Cathay by the north. They were wondering whether Greenland joined with Norway at the north, or whether there was a strait there, and some one present told the story of the Indians who, a long time before, had been storm-driven to the coast of Germany ; whereupon the stranger turned and related the substance of a conversation he had held with Cabot at Seville. He told them that, having been at Seville some years previously, he had called on their own countryman, Cabot, to learn from his lips the truth of these matters. If this guest's memory was good, and Ramusio correctly reported him, Cabot not only suppressed that which was true, but suggested that which was false. He said that his father died at the time when the news of Columbus's discovery reached England. That was untrue, for the second letters patent were made out solely to his father in 1498. He told him that he (Sebastian) first proposed the expedition to king Henry VII., another plain falsehood. He told him that the expedition was in 1496, an error of a year. He conveyed the impression that the whole series of events happened after his father's death, and made himself the sole originator and commander of the expedition, which was clearly false. He said that he found land on a westerly course; that has been shown to be true of the first expedition, but he suppresses the fact that there were two, and that not he but his father found the land. He adds to this westerly landfall an exploration as far as 56° north and Florida on the south, whereas in the short period of three months it was impossible that such an extensive voyage could have been made. He said that when he returned to England there was great confusion because of a war with Scotland, whereas the war with Scotland had been concluded by a seven years' truce in 1497, and the second expedition sailed in 1498. He stated that the voyage was not repeated on account of the confusion caused by rebellion, whereas the rebellion was quelled in 1497, and in 1498 the pretended Richard of York was a prisoner in the Tower. He said that he went to Spain at that time, whereas he did not go until 1512, fourteen years later; and he stated that he took service under Ferdinand and Isabella, while Isabella died in 1504, eight years before he removed to Spain. If Cabot had said there were two voyages, and if he had mentioned John Cabot's name, the guest would probably have remembered it, and Ramusio would have recorded facts so salient.

The account given by Gomara is short, and it also attributes to Sebastian Cabot the sole conception and conduct of the enterprise. Gomara knows of one voyage only, and that was the voyage in 1498. It was a northern voyage, "by way of Iceland"; and the continuous daylight, the immense masses of ice, and the number of men (three hundred) taken leave no room for doubt.

In Galvano's "Discourse of the World," before cited, the two voyages are also confused into one; although, as he wrote in 1563, he followed previous writers, excepting in the latitude of the landfall, and did not, like his predecessors, take his information from Sebastian Cabot. In one version of the Portuguese text, that used by Hakluyt, John Cabot's name even appears; but the indefatigable Harrisse has turned up an original copy which does not contain it, so Hakluyt would appear to have had another edition or to have glossed his original from other authorities.

I have now gone over all the authorities for the second voyage. Their testimony is irreconcilable in many respects, but, nevertheless, some firm ground can be found. These points are established: That the expedition was a large and important one; that it sailed to the north, and that the landfall was far in the north in a region of ice and continual daylight; that from the extreme north it coasted south to latitude 38° in search of an open ocean to Cathay; that having been provisioned for a year, the expedition was fitted for such an exploration, and had the time to perform it.

There is, beside the above, a passage from Fabyan's "Chronicle," cited in Stow's "Chronicle," published in 1580, and, with variations, copied into Hakluyt's "Divers Voyages," published in 1582; but, on reference to all the editions of Fabyan now extant, not only can the originals of these citations not be found, but no mention whatever of the Cabots is made. I have referred the consideration of this matter to appendix C. The passage contains no additional particulars of importance.

VII. MAPS AND MAP DRAWING IN THE 16TH CENTURY.

In Hakluyt's time there was at Westminster, in the private gallery of the queen, a copy of a map attributed to Sebastian Cabot engraved by (or under the supervision of)

Clement Adams, which indicated the landfall of the first voyage. Hakluyt has preserved the inscription but the map has disappeared with all other papers and maps from Cabot's hand. The inscription preserved by Hakluyt is found, in substance, upon the world map of 1544 (see appendix H) as well as elsewhere, but, at present, I have to do with the map Hakluyt saw. No doubt there were upon this lost map other inscriptions (as on the map of 1544) of the nature of notes giving information as to the different parts of the world portrayed upon it. That one pertaining to the subject, translated from the original Latin, is as follows:

"In the year of our Lord 1497 John Cabot a Venetian and Sebastian his son opened "up this country which no one had previously attempted to go to, upon the 24th day of "June, early in the morning about five o'clock.

"Moreover he called this land—*terram primam visam*—I believe, because he first from "sea-wards had set eyes upon that region.

"And, as there is an island situated opposite, he called it the island of St. John, I "think, for the reason that it was discovered upon St. John the Baptist's day."

The inscription on the map was in Latin and the above is a close translation. Hakluyt gives an English translation ("Principal Navigations") but he has inserted explanatory glosses. (See appendix H.)

Then follows a description, not certainly of the island, but of the whole region, Labrador included. There is a colon and the next word, *Hujus*, commences with a capital letter. *Hujus* must refer to the country generally; for, if not, there would be no description of the country, but only of that one island, and it would have been irrational for the writer to have branched off into a dissertation upon an accessory point; as absurd as it would be to commence to describe Canada and confine the description to Anticosti. This view is confirmed by the corresponding Latin inscription on the Paris map of 1544, where it is given *Hujus terræ incolæ*, &c. Then follows immediately a description of the inhabitants, their dress and mode of living and of making war, a description of the soil, of the animals on land and the fishes in the sea. It has however been shown, in a previous part of this paper, that on the first voyage Cabot saw no man. The description therefore is a general one applicable to all that region as explored afterwards by successive voyagers up to the date of the map. It is therefore unnecessary to inquire whether white bears ever existed in Cape Breton or Prince Edward island; they existed in Labrador which is sufficient. Nor is it necessary to allocate the great abundance of fishes at any one spot. The description is applicable to the whole region—to Newfoundland and Labrador as well as to Cape Breton. Only the *prima vista* is indicated specially, and opposite to it, so near that it was discovered the same day, was an island. The Paris map of 1544 says a *large* island but Clement Adams's map merely says it was an island, and he adds that on the island were hawks as black as crows, black eagles and partridges. I think this inscription has been misunderstood to apply strictly to the landfall and the island at the time of discovery.

Nevertheless the landfall was marked by an island opposite, which was named St. John's island. By opposite—*ex adverso*—cannot be meant an island 100 miles off. Some idea of adjacency must be intended. My task therefore will be to examine all the extant maps and see if they bear any evidence of a probable landfall identified by an island called St. John. The maps however are in many cases strangely distorted and before taking them up some preliminary inquiries are requisite.

Mr. Harrisse, until the publication of his " Discovery of North America " in 1892, used to maintain that the Spanish and Portuguese governments were very jealous of imparting to foreigners any information concerning their colonial enterprises and discoveries, and in that belief all other writers concurred and still concur. Moreover, it agrees with all that is known of the manners and methods of that period, and especially with the genius of those two governments." This last volume, however,[12] gives a kaleidoscopic turn to the whole picture. We are now informed that map-making was freely taught in Spain and practised by all ; that there was no tendency, at any time, to concentrate map-making in the hands of government ; that Spain never made a secret of its maritime discoveries ; that any one might buy the official charts. The general impression conveyed is that these governments, while they had colleges of cosmographers and official standard charts, were no more chary of disseminating their manuscript maps than the British Admiralty and the United States Hydrographical Survey are now. ‾ It is impossible to follow Mr. Harrisse in this new departure. His own learned researches forbid it. When Robert Thorne, resident in Seville in 1527,[83] sent a map to the English ambassador, he was careful to add " that it is not to be showed " or communicated there " (in England) " with many of that court. For though there is " nothing in it prejudiciall to the emperor, yet it may be a cause of paine to the maker ; as " well for that none may make these cardes but certayne appointed and allowed for masters." The patent fact exists that no maps of these discoveries were printed in Spain ; all the Spanish maps are in manuscript. The exceptions of the small map of the West Indies found in a few copies of an edition of Peter Martyr in 1511, and the sketch map in Medina's " Arte di Navegar " in 1545, prove the rule ; for in 1511 an edict was issued forbidding the communication of charts to foreigners, and the later and complete editions of Martyr are without the map. Columbus in 1503 seized all the maps in the possession of his crew. In 1527 an edict was issued by Charles V. excluding all strangers from the positions of pilot or mate. It could not have been a mere form, when the official charts were kept in a coffer with two locks, one of which was kept by the pilot major and the other by the junior cosmographer. The Portuguese government decreed the penalty of death to any one who should communicate a map of their discoveries in the east. It is irrational to suppose that no restrictions existed in other directions. These facts cannot be explained away, and they are important to remember, or we shall not be able to account for the intermittent character of the progress of geographical knowledge as shown upon the maps.

Another important point to be borne in mind is that the sailors of those days sailed by dead reckoning. They had no means of checking their longitudes, while their latitudes might be fairly accurate. Distorted as the maps may appear, there is, however, on American maps one point clear and unmistakable, which serves as a point of reference, namely, Cape Race. It is the pole star of the early maps, as it still is and always has been the great beacon of the ocean highway. The name appears first on the King chart as Cape Raso about the year 1502, and as Raz, Razzo, Rasso, and in our English corrupted form *Race* it has persisted to the present day. The name signifies the " flat cape," and whoever gave so suitable a name must have seen the locality.

The distortion of some of these early maps is, however, due to a much more influential cause, and I should not have ventured to treat of so difficult a matter if I had not had the shelter of so great an authority as Champlain. At the present day maps are drawn to their true meridian, irrespective of the magnetic meridian. This is indicated by a subsidiary point or by a note. The card of the mariner's compass is now so attached that the *fleur-de-lis* is over the north pole of the needle, and always indicates the magnetic north, and as a vessel sails from one magnetic zone to another the local variation is obtained from the charts and allowed for in the course steered. In these early days now under review the science of magnetism was undreamed of, and the magnetic variation was almost uniform throughout Europe at one point east of north. No observations existed then as now, and only in 1492 had the variation from east to west first been noticed. Sailors in those days sailed each on the compass corrected for his own country, and the card was attached with the *fleur-de-lis*, not over the pole of the needle, but over that point west of it which was conceived to be the true north; for the needle, to adopt Champlain's word, *easted*. But when the needle crossed over and *wested* a point or a point and a-half, the two quantities of variation were added and the *fleur-de-lis* pointed two or two and a-half points west of north," and the west point was therefore two and a-half points south of west, and consequently the continual tendency of vessels, as elsewhere stated, was to drop to the south on a westerly course. In order to obviate this tendency they did not change the compasses, but the sailing charts were so drawn as to throw up the coast to the required degree of northing to correspond with the lay of the compass-card. Hence upon a sailing chart the east point of Cape Breton would be represented due west of Cape Race, whereas it is really a full point south of it.

As an illustration of the confusion which has crept into this question, from not noticing this peculiarity of the old sailing charts, I would cite Kohl (" Doc. His.," p. 178); he is discussing Reinel's chart of 1505, and he says that " there is one indication of latitude along a " perpendicular line, and another indication along an oblique or transverse line which is " shorter. This latter line is nearer the truth, and perhaps was added to the map by a later " hand." But Reinel meant to indicate that his map was drawn on the meridian shown by the compass of his own country, and that it was twenty degrees or nearly two points out. The oblique line is the true meridian, and if it be placed to point north the east point of Cape Breton will be not west of Cape Race but about true west-southwest.

In order to put this matter beyond doubt I have translated the chapter of Champlain (see appendix A) in which he explains the two maps at the end of his voyages of 1613. The text explains the principle and the maps illustrate it. The small map is drawn to its true meridian and the large map is drawn to the compass in use by sailors, which was set to the variation of France. On this latter map the coast, from Cape Race to Cape Breton east point, is shown as lying east and west, as in the maps of Juan de la Cosa and Reinel and very many others. On this map also is shown the oblique line which Kohl supposed a later hand had added to Reinel's map. If a line be drawn from 47°, the latitude of Cape Race, at right angles to that shorter line, the latitude on the marginal line will coincide.

Bearing in mind the preceding considerations, the study of the early maps will become much more profitable, and I would now direct attention to them to ascertain what light they may throw upon the landfall of John Cabot and the island of St. John opposite to it. It must be remembered that John Cabot took the time to go on shore at his landfall and planted the banners of England and St. Mark there. At that time of year and in that latitude it was light at half-past three, but it was five when he saw land, and he had to reach it and perform the ceremonies appropriate for such occasions; so the island opposite could not be far away. The island, then, will be useful to identify the landfall if we find it occurring frequently on the succeeding maps.

Juan de la Cosa—A. D. 1500.

Juan de la Cosa's Map, A.D. 1500. Don Pedro de Ayala, joint Spanish ambassador at London, wrote, on July 25th, 1498, to his sovereigns that he had procured and would send a copy of John Cabot's chart of his first voyage. This map of Juan de la Cosa is evidence that Ayala fulfilled his promise. It is a manuscript map [52] made at the end of the year 1500, by the eminent Biscayan pilot who, if not the equal of Columbus in nautical and cosmographical knowledge, was easily the second to him. Upon it there is a continuous coast-line from Labrador to Florida showing that the claim made by Sebastian Cabot of having coasted from a region of ice and snow to the latitude of Gibraltar was accepted as true by La Cosa, whatever later Spanish writers may have said. Recent writers of authority have arrived at the conclusion that, immediately after Columbus and Cabot had opened the way, many independent adventurers visited the western seas ; for there are a number of geographical facts recorded on the earliest charts not easy to account for on any other hypothesis. Dr. Justin Winsor shows that La Cosa, and others of the great sailors of the earliest years of discovery, soon recognized that they had encountered a veritable barrier to Asia consisting of islands, or an island of continental size, through which they had to find a passage to the golden east. Their views were not however generally accepted, and it soon got to be a maxim of the schools, *Quicquid præter Africam et Europam est, Asia est.* Without however stopping to discuss this point I would again call attention to the fact that the coast line is continuous. If, as Stevens and Humboldt thought, Cabot had made a periplus of the gulf of St. Lawrence—if he had got embayed in our waters—if he had sailed round Prince Edward island (and beyond question he could never have suspected it to be an island unless he had sailed round it)—if he had sailed along the north shore of the St. Lawrence from Quebec to the straits of Belle-Isle and thence into the ocean and proved Newfoundland to be an immense island—it is impossible but that some trace of so remarkable an achievement should have been recorded on some early map. On this map there is no lurking place for Prince Edward island—no gulf—no inner sea—and what islands are laid down are very small and are in the ocean. That La Cosa based the northern part of his map upon Cabot's discoveries is demonstrated by the English flags marked along the coast and the legend, *Mar descubierto por Ingleses ;* because no English but the Cabot expeditions had been there ; and what is evidently intended for Cape Race is called *Cavo de Ynglaterra.* The English flags mark off the coast from that cape to what may be considered as Cape Hatteras. Cabot, as before stated, confidently expected to reach Cathay. He sailed for that as his objective point and he was looking for a broad western ocean, so that narrow openings were to him simply bays of greater or less depth. The sailors of those early voyages coasted from headland to headland as plainly appears from many of the maps upon which the recesses of the sinuosities of the coast are not completed lines, and it must be borne in mind that in sailing between Newfoundland and Cape Breton the bold and peculiar contours of both can be seen at the same time. This is possible in anything like clear weather, but, in the bright weather of midsummer day, Cape Ray would necessarily have been seen from St. Paul's and the opening might well have been taken for a deep indentation of the coast. Between *Cavo descubierto* and *Cavo St. Jorge* such an indentation is shown on the map but the line is closed showing that Cabot did not sail through.

In studying this remarkable map attention is at once aroused by the fact that from *Cavo de Ynglaterra* to *Cavo descubierto* the coast is continuously named. In other words that the south coast of Newfoundland is named, but not the east coast ; whereas, in Reinel's map five years later, the east coast is named but not the south and Reinel's names are Portuguese, many of which still cling to the localities [51] in a more or less corrupted form. It is very unlikely that, sailing 2,000 miles over an utterly unknown sea, Cabot should have made precisely the point of Cape Race. It is made always now, but it is aimed at. To suppose Cabot hit it is like supposing a man to make a chance-medley shot across a rifle range in a fog and to hit the bull's-eye. It is within the limit of possibility but the chances are many thousands to one it will not be done. Now on looking at the row of names on La Cosa's map it will be seen that they commence with Cape of England (*Cavo de Yngla-terra*) on the east point and stop with *Cavo descubierto* on the west. At one of these two points the discovery must have been made and the coasting commenced. Either Cabot exactly hit Cape Race and coasted westward to Cape Discovery, or he discovered land at Cape Discovery and, his object having been attained and his provisions falling short, he turned and coasted eastwards giving the name Cape of England to the last spot of western land he saw as he set his course on the return voyage to England. When we consider the force of the names themselves we feel that the latter alternative must be the true one, and Juan de la Cosa's map therefore becomes conclusive evidence for the priority of the flag of England on the northeastern coast of the North American continent. John Cabot must have been very clear in his report, because Raimondo di Soncino in his second letter [70] to the Duke of Milan says that Cabot had constructed a globe and had pointed out the place where he had been. This was in the winter between the two voyages so that no confusion between them was possible.

Cavo descubierto!—the discovered cape—and close to it, *Mar descubierto por Ingleses!* What can be more evident than that the spot where Europeans first touched the American continent is thus indicated? Why otherwise should it especially be called "the discovered cape" if not because this cape was first discovered? It is stated elsewhere that on the same day, opposite the land, an island was also discovered; and in fact upon the Madrid fac-simile two small islands are found, one of which is near *Cavo descubierto*. The name *the discovered cape* at the extreme end of a series of names tells its own story. Cabot overran Cape Race and went south of St. Pierre and Miquelon without seeing them, and continuing on a westerly course hit Cape Breton at its most easterly point. An apt illustration occurs in a voyage made by the ship "Bonaventure" in 1591 recorded in Hakluyt. She overshot Cape Race without knowing it and came to the soundings on the bank [51] south of St. Peter's, where they found 20 fathoms, and then the course was set N. W. by N., for Cape Ray. The course was sharply altered towards a definite and known point but, if he did not see Cape Race, not knowing what was before him Cabot would have had no object in abruptly alter-ing his course but, continuing his westerly course, would strike the east point of Cape Breton. That point then, and not Cape North, would be the "discovered cape"—the *prima vista*—and there not far off "over against the land" "opposite the land" (*ex adverso*) he would find Scatari island which would be the island of St. John so continually attendant on Cape Breton upon the succeeding maps. If this theory be accepted all becomes clear, and the little *Matthew*, having achieved success, having demonstrated the existence of Cathay within easy reach of England returned home; noticing and naming the salient features of the south coast of Newfoundland. She had not too much time to do it, for she was back in Bristol in 34 days at most. This theory is further confirmed by the circumstance recorded by Pasqualigo that as Cabot returned he saw two islands on the right, which he had not time to examine being short of provisions. These islands would be St. Pierre and Miquelon ; for there are two, and only two, important islands possible to be seen at the right on the south coast of Newfoundland on the homeward course. La Cosa beside the two small islands above noted has marked on his map three larger islands, I. de la Trinidad, S. Grigor, and I. Verde but they are not laid down on the map in the places of St. Pierre and Miquelon nor are there any islands existing in the positions shown. I. de la Trinidad is doubtless the peninsula of Burin, as would appear by its position almost in contact with the land and its very peculiar shape. In coasting along it would appear as an island for the isthmus is very narrow, and St. Pierre and Miquelon would be clearly seen as islands on the right. As for the bearings of the coast it will appear by a comparison with Champlain's large map that they are compass bearings for they are the same on both.

I have dwelt at length upon the map of La Cosa because, for our northern coasts, it is in effect John Cabot's map. After the return of the second expedition, the English made a few voyages but soon fell back into the old rut of their Iceland trade. The expedition was beyond question a commercial failure, and therefore, like the practical people they are, they neglected that new continent which was destined to become the chief theatre for the expansion of their race. Their fishermen were for many years to be found in small numbers only on the coast, and, as before, their supply of codfish was drawn from Iceland where they could sell goods in exchange.

Meantime the Bretons and Normans, and the Basques of France and Spain, and the Portuguese, grasped that which England practically abandoned. That landfall which Cabot gave her in 1497 cost much blood and treasure to win back in 1758. The French fishermen were on the coast as early as 1504, and the names on La Cosa's map were displaced by French names still surviving on the south coast and on what is called the French shore of Newfoundland. Robert Thorne in 1527 (and no doubt others unrecorded) in vain urged upon the English Government to vindicate its right. According to the papal bulls and the treaty of Tordesillas the new lands were Portuguese east of a meridian 370 leagues west of the Cape de Verde islands and Spanish to the west of it. Baccalaos and Labrador were considered to be Portuguese and, upon the maps, when any mention is made of English discoveries they are accordingly relegated to Greenland or the far north of Labrador. The whole claim of England went by abandonment and default. The Portuguese as the Rev. Dr. Patterson has shown, named all the east coast of Newfoundland and their traces are even yet found on the coasts of Nova Scotia and of Cape Breton.

Therefore it is that the maps we have now to refer to are not so much Spanish as Portuguese. They will tell us nothing of the English, nor of Cabot, but we shall be able to follow his island of St. John—the only one of his names which survived. The outlines of some very early maps are given by Kunstmann, Kretschmer and Winsor, but until 1505 they have no bearing upon our problem. In that year Reinel's map was made, and although Newfoundland forms part of *terra firma*, the openings north and south of it are plainly indicated by unclosed lines. Cape Race has received its permanent name *Raso* and although only the east coast of Newfoundland is named there is no possibility of mistaking the easternmost point of Cape Breton. Just opposite, (*ex adverso*) is laid down and named the island of Sam Joha, in lat. 46°, the precise latitude of Scatari island. Here, then, in 1505 is in this island of St. John an independent testimony to the landfall of 1497—not off Cape North, which does not yet appear, nor inside the gulf for it is not even indicated—but in the

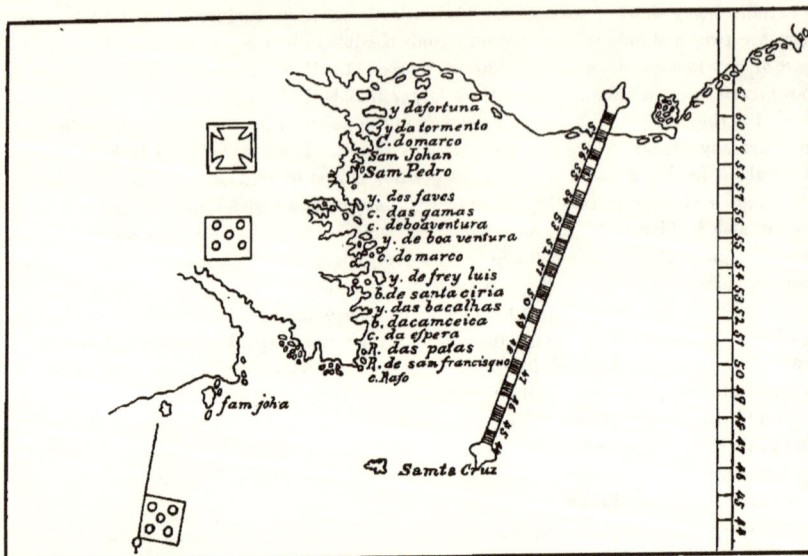

Pedro Reinel, A.D. 1505 (from Kohl).

Atlantic ocean, at the cape of Cape Breton [73]—the *cavo descubierto* of La Cosa. All La Cosa's names are omitted. This map of Reinel is very accurately drawn and is evidently based on direct and original knowledge. The island he lays down is not of the conventional shape but triangular like Scatari. We shall find the triangular island he placed at 46 degrees will

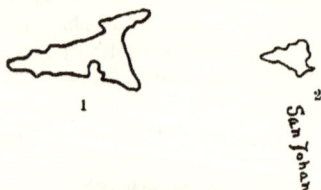

1. Outline of Scatari Island on a large scale from Gisborne's Map.

2. Outline of Sam Joha from Kretschmer on a larger scale than Kohl's facsimile.

persist there. It may not retain its correct shape. It may move a little further out or may deviate somewhat from the true latitude; but always we shall find it, with or without its name, in the ocean opposite—*ex adverso*—the easternmost point of Cape Breton. We shall find, for a long time, subsequent maps not so accurate, but for forty years upon the majority of maps an island, which when named will be called the island of S. Johan, Joa, Joha,[77] Joam, will be found to attend upon that point of land. The straits will be closed up north and south and Cape Breton and Newfoundland will be welded firmly to the mainland; but St. John's island will remain in the ocean where Cabot found it, until, in the map of 1544, some one, availing himself of the information upon the French maps, attached that name to the Magdalen group which Cartier had discovered in 1534; not to Prince Edward island as of late commonly supposed.

Harrisse in discussing this question (throughout his work on the Cabots) is perplexed by his theory, based on the erroneous reading of the map of 1544, that Prince Edward is the island of St. John; and asks how it is possible, in that case, that Newfoundland should for so long a time after appear as part of the firm land. There is no answer to his question but one. It is impossible; and any theory identifying Cabot's St. John with Prince Edward island will lead to endless contradictions. It may be observed here, however, that about 1520 there began to appear, south of Cape Race and often in the same meridian, an imaginary island of St. John Estevan; one of those flying islands which had no real existence and which disappeared off the maps about A.D. 1600. This must not be confounded with the island of St. John opposite the east point of Cape Breton often marked on the same maps with it.

The next map having relation to the subject is Ruysch's found in the Ptolemy published at Rome in 1508 and the first *printed* map containing any notice of America. Cape Race is called Cabo di Portugesi; Labrador, Newfoundland and Greenland are parts of the solid continent of Asia and the great Southern ocean joins the Atlantic and separates them from the Spanish discoveries at the south, but a deep bay marks the separation of Newfoundland from Cape Breton, and off a point south of the bay a little island (Biggetu—a name never occurring again) keeps the place of St. John.[80]

The same mark of the landfall appears on a map in Kunstmann's atlas. It is assigned to the date of A.D. 1514-20. This follows Reinel's type and indicates by unclosed lines the passages north and south of Newfoundland. The coasts are however part of the solid continent. Off the extreme point marking Cape Breton is a legend stating that it was discovered by the Bretons and opposite to it in the ocean is a small island, unnamed, marking the place of St. John's island of Reinel. In 1527 Robert Thorne sent a map to the English ambassador as previously observed. It is valuable only as vindicating for the English the same extent of coast as was marked by English flags on La Cosa's map—a claim which Sebastian Cabot, then also at Seville as pilot major to Spain, was letting go to Portugal without one recorded remonstrance.

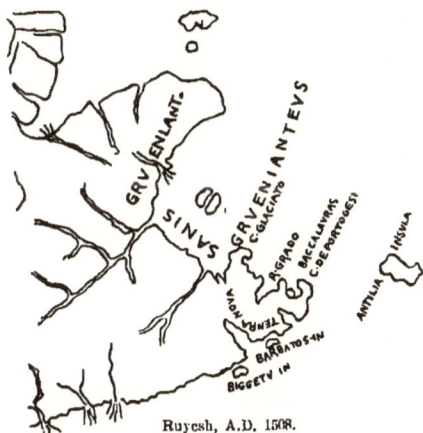

Ruysch, A.D. 1508.

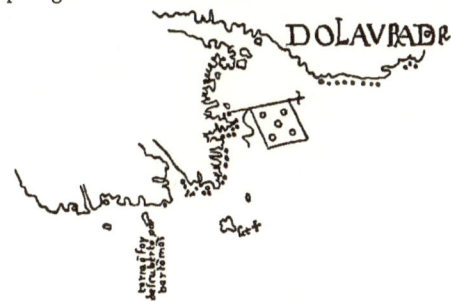

A.D. 1514-20 (from Kunstmann.)

The next map calling for notice is a very important one in the Ambrosian library at Milan. It is by Vescoute de Maggiolo and is dated 1527. We still have the contour of a solid continent and, in the ocean, south and opposite to C. de Bertoni is the I. de S. Juan in its proper place and named. Neither the gulf nor Cape North are indicated. This map is plate XIV. of Kretschmer's collection. The French flag now begins to appear, showing evidences of Verrazano's presence on the coast of New England and the Middle states. The

Vesconte de Maggiolo, A.D. 1527.

official map of Ribero made at Seville in 1529 does not show an island near Cape Breton but no sign of the gulf of St. Lawrence appears upon it.

In the same year 1529, was made the celebrated mappemonde of Hieronimus de Verrazano now in the Propaganda at Rome. It embodies the claims based upon his brother's voyage in 1523 and the whole coast of New England, which Cabot in 1498 had sailed along, is marked with French flags. The southern opening into the gulf is widened and named G. di St. Joanne and, in this single instance, north of the east point of Cape

Verrazano, A.D. 1529.

Breton is marked Isla de Sancto Joanni, but still there are no signs of any knowledge of the gulf of St. Lawrence. The Ptolemy of 1530 Basle Ed., shows Cape Breton with its satellite still in the Atlantic but the coast is a continuous line; nor does the least sign of the gulf appear upon the globe of Orontius Finæus in 1531.

We have arrived at the year 1531, thirty-four years after Cabot's first voyage, and while the island of St. John has been indicated it is always in the Atlantic and in close contiguity with what would appear to be the landfall of 1497, namely the east point of Cape Breton. We have found openings to the north and south of Newfoundland but they lead nowhere and sometimes the lines are closed at a greater or less depth and the coast is continuous. The gulf of St. Lawrence is, so far, non-existent and Prince Edward island is yet unborn into the world.

Fishermen were, however, moving all around the coast. A map in the Ptolemy of 1511, although most fragmentary and incomplete, seems to indicate a vague knowledge of the

Gaspar Viegas, A. D. 1534.

Grand Bay in the north at an early period. It was there that Cartier found the port of Brest on his first voyage. A frequented port evidently; because he met on the coast a vessel from Rochelle looking for it. The Portuguese were then working more on the east coast of Newfoundland and to the south at Cape Breton and Nova Scotia, for in 1534 the gulf of St. Lawrence commenced to appear in embryo upon a group of Portuguese maps; and that same year Jacques Cartier sailed into it through the straits of Belle-Isle. Of this group of maps Viegas' (1534) is a type, showing a small round gulf with a few rivers opening into it.

Viegas' map separates Cape Breton island from the mainland by a narrow strait and Cape Breton, the headland itself, is the neighbouring point of Nova Scotia now Cape Canso, and there is, out in the ocean off the coast, a small island called do Breta. A map in an atlas in

Portuguese Map from Kretschmer.

the Riccardiana library at Florence given in *Kretschmer* as plate XXXIII. illustrates this by naming the island of Cape Breton (unnamed in Viegas') as Sam Joa. From Harrisse's description of the Wolfenbuttel map of 1534[50] the same features are shown upon it. These maps display a much fuller knowledge of the coast around the strait of Canso; while to the north, Newfoundland still forms part of the solid continent. In commenting upon them Harrisse falls into an error resulting, probably, from his not having sailed in those waters or studied them on local maps of large scale. He is unable to recognize the square island at the mouth of the gulf as Cape Breton island, because the passage between it and

the mainland is marked as running north and south, whereas he says the strait of Canso lies east and west ; moreover, he thinks that any one sailing through the strait could not fail at once to see Prince Edward island.   This very north and south direction of the strait is, to a Canadian, an evidence of knowledge, for, although Chedabucto bay has its greater axis east and west, the strait of Canso lies exactly north and south by the compass or true N.N.W. and S.S.E.. and on passing in, by the Lennox or by the southern channel from the ocean, there is a sharp and sudden turn to the right at Bear island, which is probably the cause why the through passage was so long concealed.   The strait is only a mile wide, and the bold outline of Cape Porcupine interlocking with the high lands of the opposite coast bar the view and form an apparent bay.   In old days it was the resort of vessels seeking concealment, and the railway ferry is near a place formerly called Pirate's harbour.   Again, because of that very north and south direction a vessel might continue on a straight course north to the Magdalens or Labrador, without suspecting the existence of Prince Edward island.   The coast of Cape Breton is lofty, but that of Prince Edward island is very low and cannot be seen further than twenty miles in the very clearest weather, and, if seen, would be taken as part of the mainland, because of the interlocking headlands of Nova Scotia and the high lands in rear of them.   These are points which Mr. Harrisse may well be excused for missing from defect of that intimate knowledge which those very much inferior to him in learning may obtain by familiarity with the localities.   One point must still be noted, that, although in these Portuguese maps the gulf has commenced to reveal itself, no islands are shown in it, and Prince Edward island will yet remain for sixty years firmly adherent to the mainland in all succeeding maps.

The voyages of Jacques Cartier open a new era in the geography of the northeast coast of America.   They have been so thoroughly elucidated by Canadian writers, notably by Ferland, Laverdière, Ganong and Pope,[36] that scarcely anything remains to be said. Cartier sailed to the northern entrance of the gulf confidently, as to a well-known place, and passed into the expanse between Newfoundland and Labrador, then, and long after,

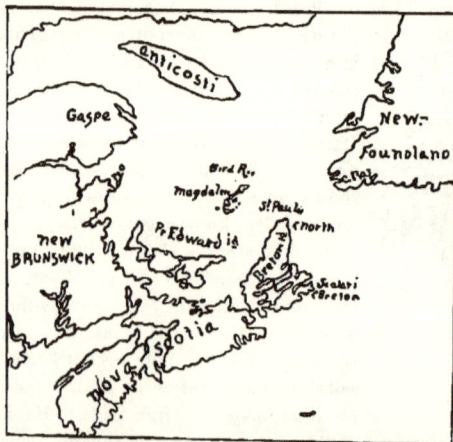

Map of the Gulf of St. Lawrence to show the relative position of Prince Edward and the Magdalen Islands.

called *La Grande Baye.* He found the coasts named, and the harbour of Brest (now Old Fort bay) a well known rendezvous of fishermen from France. He passed through *La Grande Baye* and sailed into the main gulf. As well shown by Pope and Ganong, he sailed across it, discovering the islands in his course (the Magdalen group including Brion island and the Bird rocks), and he touched at the north point of Prince Edward island, without recognizing it as an island.   For, in fact, as is well known to those who have sailed in those waters, the long projecting capes of the island and of the adjacent provinces of New Brunswick and Nova Scotia so overlap that capes Egmont and Tormentine seem to inclose a large bay.   It is not strange, then, that Cartier passed on westward to the New Brunswick coast without suspecting the existence of Northumberland strait.   Any one who has crossed to Summerside and to Charlottetown will have observed how the island lies, as it were, in the lap of the sister provinces, and all sailors know, what in fact is evident upon the chart, that it is far out of the way of vessels sailing into the gulf by any entrance but the strait of Canso.   The entire coast is low and not visible at any great distance, and it is not surprising that for sixty years after Cartier the existence of the separating strait of Northumberland is unrecorded, and without doubt was unsuspected.

Cartier's two voyages attracted no attention in Spain ; but the preparations of Roberval in 1540 were jealously watched by spies and reported to the Emperor Charles V. Finding that the expedition was destined for some part of Baccalaos, he endeavoured to incite the Portuguese to follow [57] and crush it.   That part of America had fallen to Portugal under the bull of demarcation, and the French were looked upon as trespassers ; but Portugal was not in a position to take such high ground as Spain.   Gomez, in 1525, is the only Spaniard who is recorded as having sailed along our coasts in these early years.

In 1536 the Spanish *Padron Real,* or standard official map, would seem to have fallen into arrears, and Charles V. commissioned Alonzo de Chaves to include all the latest discoveries and bring it down to date.   The map which resulted from his labours has been lost ; but Oviedo has given so detailed a description of it that it might almost be reproduced.   It contained the results of Gomez' explorations, and upon it was traced the strait of Canso under the name of the passage of St. Julian.   The point of Cape Breton is noted as being upon the island of St. John, and this transfer of the name St. John from the small satellite island to the larger one will be found repeated later in several important maps. Gomez gives the size of the island as 56 leagues long by 20 leagues wide, and in passing it he said that he saw much smoke, which led him to think it was inhabited.   This little observation gives reality to the narrative ; for the appearance of Smoky Cape—Cape Enfumé —(Baia des Fumos of the Portuguese)—is very remarkable, and might well mislead any stranger sailing along the coast.   With singular reiteration Harrisse insists, even against this clear evidence, upon pronouncing the island of St. John to be fictitious like the islands of Santa Cruz and St. Brandan.   His objections are based, as pointed out previously, upon misconceptions arising from want of local knowledge of the gulf and its approaches. Enough is recorded of De Chaves' map to show that, for him, the island of Cape Breton was, itself, the island of St. John.

Whatever the Portuguese (appendix E) may have done on the Atlantic coast, to the French is due the entire credit of revealing the gulf of St. Lawrence.   In the wake of Cartier followed Bretons, Normans, and Basques, both French and Spanish, but it was long before his discoveries passed into the maps.   The map of Agnese (1536), that of Munster (1540), that of Mercator (1541), and the Ulpius globe of 1542 show no indication of the gulf of St. Lawrence ; but all show the east point of Cape Breton and its satellite island in the Atlantic, evidently the St. John of former and later maps.   The delusion that America was, at the north, a part of eastern Asia died hard.   It lingered on until about 1548, when it may still be found in Ptolemy.   The great western ocean was supposed to wash the southern shores of a vast northern continent stretching from Cathay to Baccalaos, and it was therefore called the Great South sea.[58]   The name lingers still in our ordinary speech ; for

when we call the seal-skins which come from Behring's sea *South sea seal* we are uncon-
sciously re-echoing the delusions of three hundred years ago. But the dream that this great
southern ocean swept far eastwards and inwards towards the Atlantic in a great bay was
dominant in Cartier's day, and for more than a hundred and twenty years after. In some maps
it seems to reach within a hundred miles of the Atlantic coast; sometimes in the latitudes of
the Carolinas, and sometimes further north. No wonder Cartier sailed up our great river
expecting every headland would reveal the great secret. Jolliet paddled down the western
rivers with the same hope. Lake after lake raised the same anticipations as they opened out
their wondrous chain; and even still, in these prosaic times, in imagination we can picture
the figure of the brooding La Salle gazing wistfully over the waters of our familiar Lake St.
Louis, where it stretches away to the west from the bluff bank of his seigniory, at the rise
of the road near the present village of Lachine.

By the year 1542 the contour of the gulf began to get into the maps, and the map of
Rotz [57] of that year shows the whole outline of the gulf and the strait of Canso, but no indication of Northumberland strait. The *globe* of Rotz (A.D. 1543) is the first to show the Magda-

Rotz, A. D. 1542.

len group, but it does not show Prince Edward island. The
peculiar curve, concave to the east, and the lay of the island
marked, as well as its situation in the direct course through
the gulf, render a mistake impossible. The Vallard map of
1543 shows the same group changed in shape, but Ganong's
reasons for identifying it with the great Magdalen are unan-
swerable. [58] The island of Cape Breton is drawn out of place
and made to lie parallel with the coast of Nova Scotia, a distortion repeated on a few later maps; among others, on the
mappemonde Harleyenne, as described by Mr. Harrisse. [59]
In that map, however, Cape Breton island is called the island
of St. Johan—a transfer of name from the satellite to the main island (appendix D) occurring likewise in the rhymed routier of Jean Allefonsce by Mallart, as well as in that compiled by Secalart, but still retaining the island on the Atlantic coast. By the year 1543
the gulf had received on Vallard's map the name of Rio de Canada. The Spaniards called
it Golfo Quadrado (the square gulf); and yet Prince Edward island had not been developed
on the maps, while we find the island of St. John still in the Atlantic, whether the name
be attached to the large or the small island, and wherever the words Cape Breton are found
a small island is always near (*ex adverso*).

The celebrated "Cabot" map of 1544 would come in here in order of date; but I pass
it for the present, and proceed to the Dauphin map of 1546. This map has a paramount
interest to Canadians, for upon it first appear the names Canada, Ochelaga, Saguay,
L'Assomption, Belle Isle, Franciroy. It was drawn by Pierre Deceliers, at Arques, a town
which is almost a suburb of Dieppe, the centre of maritime activity in Normandy, [61] and its
author was a contemporary of Jacques Cartier. For the present inquiry the chief importance of this map is the delineation of the island which Cartier discovered in the gulf, and
which, in the so-called Cabot map of 1544, is called St. John. An inspection of this map—
a map, moreover, made in Cartier's lifetime—identifies it with the Magdalen. The name
group of islands is misleading, for the Magdalens (appendix F) consist of one large island
formed by a double line of sandbanks with three outlying islands—Entry island, in the

Dauphin, or Henry II. Map, A.D. 1516.

bosom, as it were, of the long, straggling main island, and the Bird rocks and Brion island to the northeast. This is the precise arrangement on the Dauphin map. First, Isle aux Margaulx, then Isle Brion, then the long, straggling main island, and an island in the centre which may well be Entry island. Further, at the southwest end, is Alezay, which Pope and Ganong have identified as Deadman's island. It is evident, therefore, that Jacques Cartier did not know of Prince Edward island as an island, but thought the point he touched a headland of the main shore. This group of connected islands is fifty-six miles long; it was discovered in 1534, and the compiler of the map of 1544, finding that it was being inserted in the new maps, and that it was next to the *prima vista* of Cabot, without any authority whatever and ignorant of the distance and physical facts, assumed that it was the island of St. John of the legend No. 8 of the map.

In connection with the Dauphin map, a mappemonde described by Harrisse in the British Museum, by the same Deceliers,[52] is worthy of careful consideration. It purports to embody the results of the voyages of Cartier and Roberval, and this island, which Harrisse takes to be Prince Edward island, is named *isle des arènes*—isle of sands.[63] No one who ever saw the "garden of the gulf" would call it "isle of sands," for the forest comes down to the beaches even of the northern coast.

The maps of Gastaldi, 1550—of Nicolay, 1553, and one in Ramusio of 1556, do not show the gulf. The point of Cape Breton, with its attendant island, is, however, given. Sometimes, on the maps of this period, the island is called Breton, as well as the cape. In an atlas by Guillaume le Testu, dated 1555, described by Harrisse,[61] the island inside the gulf is called *Ile Gazeas*, which he says is a corruption of Alezay, while he yet erroneously supposes it to be Prince Edward island. The map of Diego Homem, 1558, shows the island in the gulf as *ille de Sablo²s* (isle of sands—Sable island), but the position as well as the name precludes the supposition that it is Prince Edward island.

I have now gone over all the list of maps given by Harrisse in his work on the Cabots and some others besides, and Prince Edward island has not yet emerged from its hiding place in the lap of Nova Scotia; but I have continually found the island of St. John—always in the Atlantic, and always near the eastern cape of Cape Breton—the *prima vista* of John Cabot. It will, however, be well to follow down the chain of maps until our island province is born into that independent position which, in our days, it so greatly values; and, upon the Jomard map of about the same date, the gulf will be found fairly drawn, but with-

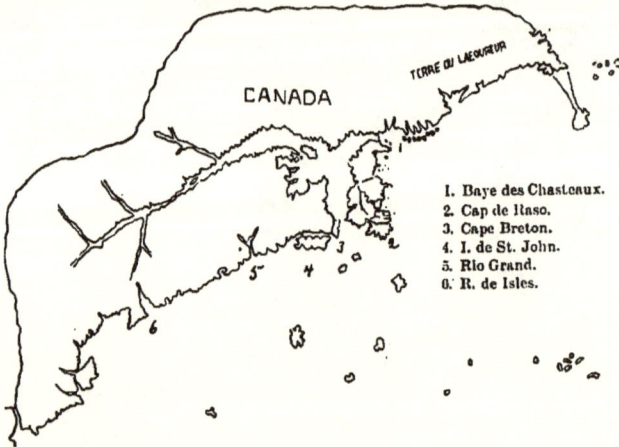

1. Baye des Chasteaux.
2. Cap de Raso.
3. Cape Breton.
4. I. de St. John.
5. Rio Grand.
6. R. de Isles.

Jomard, A.D. 155—.

out islands, while the island of St. John is marked in the Atlantic in its accustomed place. The same remark is applicable to the Bellero map of 1554. Ruscelli's map of 1561 seems to be largely drawn from imagination; but even that gives the cape with its island; but he calls the island Breston. Zaltieri's map, 1566, does the same; as also Des Liens' map of the same year, and that of Ortelius in 1570. The map of Gerard Mercator, dated 1569, is the first in our series of maps to give its present

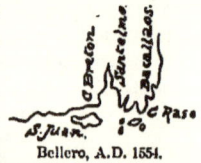

Bellero, A.D. 1554.

name to the gulf, which appears as Sinus S. Laurentii. The name which Cartier gave to a bay on the north shore was thenceforth (no one knows how) extended over the whole gulf.[61] The island in the centre reappears without a name; but now we meet a cape St. John[a] on the mainland, where Prince Edward island is to be born, and the name appears now first

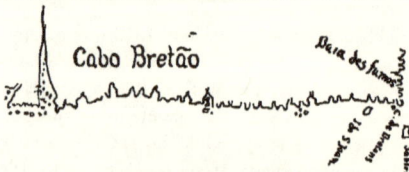

Vaz Dourado, A.D. 1573.

inside the gulf, at some point on the north coast of the still adherent Prince Edward island. Two maps by Vaz Dourado (Kunstmann, plates 10 and 11), dated between 1573-80, show the coast on a large scale. Both of them mark the island of St. John near the point of Cape Breton, and upon one we meet the name *baia des fumos* applied to the line of coast called

"Cap Enfumé"—Smoky cape. The appropriateness of the name is still manifest to the passing traveller, for the steep cliffs seem ever shrouded in a rising, smoke-like mist. Upon the other the gulf is shown, and the island, which has been taken for Prince Edward, is called isle Dorean, a Portuguese corruption of d'arènes, clearly identifying it with the sand heaps of the Magdalens. Michael Lok's map, 1582 (see *post*), in Hakluyt's "Divers Voyages," though very incorrect in many respects, is instructive, because it is the only map, excepting that of 1544, which mentions John Cabot. Upon the coast of Cape Breton is marked J. Cabot, 1497; and in the ocean near the eastern cape called C. Breton, is the island of St. John. The same position for the island is shown on the map (see *post*) in Hakluyt's "Principal Navigations," dated 1599. On the Molyneux map of 1592 it is a little further west, and more off the east coast of Nova Scotia, although several small unnamed islands appear in the gulf.

Vaz Dourado, A.D. 1573.

Thus we have come down to the year 1600, when Pontgravé, Lescarbot and, above all, Champlain are about to appear on our coasts, and save on one map, that of 1544, the island of St. John is still on the outside of Cape Breton. Prince Edward island has not yet been born upon the maps. With Champlain comes a new era. His voyages and writings, and his ever ready pencil, throw a flood of light over the obscurities of our geography. In the voyage of 1603 he embodies a description, by the Sieur Prevert of St. Malo, of the Acadian coast of the gulf, and mention is made of an island of St. John, undoubtedly our Prince Edward, for he says it is 30 to 35 leagues in length and about 6 leagues from the coast. Mention is also made of the island of Cape Breton, under the name of island of St. Lawrence; but, on his two first maps, what is now known as Prince Edward island does not appear. On the map with the Voyages of 1613 a very small island appears, marked as I. St. Jean, in the position of its northwestern point, and on the Acadian coast is a legend stating that the author had not examined the coast. Upon the map of 1632 Prince Edward island appears first in its proper place and in its full proportions, and in the volume of that date he makes a full mention of it.

From these considerations the following conclusions necessarily flow :

1. That the island called St. John on the map of 1544 is not that now known as Prince Edward island, but is the great Magdalen island, which lies in the course of vessels passing through the strait between Cape Breton and Newfoundland.

2. That the island of St. John of Cabot is Seatari island, marking the landfall at Cape Breton, the easternmost point of the island called after it, and that that cape is the natural landfall of a vessel missing Cape Race and pursuing a westerly course.

VIII. The "Cabot" Map of 1544.

In the previous part of this paper it has been shown that John Cabot made maps of his first voyage which were sent to Spain and were embodied in the map of Juan de la Cosa.

An endeavour was also made to show, quite independently of the map of 1544, that John Cabot, on his first voyage, oversailed Cape Race and made the next natural landfall, the east point of Cape Breton island.   It has been also shown that, after the sailing of the second expedition, the whole Cabot family disappeared for ever from history, excepting Sebastian alone.   He also disappears for fourteen years, when he emerges in Spain.   A few scattered indications survive of voyages meanwhile from England to the "new found islands," but he cannot be positively identified with any of them.   What he did in the interim is not known.   He probably made maps.   Suddenly, in 1512, he appears in the public accounts.   Henry VIII. had joined Ferdinand of Spain in a league against France, and was preparing an expedition to assist in an attack from Spain upon the south of France, and, in May, 1512, Sebastian Cabot was employed to make a map of Guienne and Gascony, the projected theatre of war.   Then came sudden advancement.   In September of the same year Ferdinand wrote to Lord Willoughby, the English commander, to have Cabot sent to him.   Under the same date he wrote to Cabot, inviting him to enter his service, with the object, as appears elsewhere, of consulting him concerning the navigation to Baccalaos.   In October the king allotted to Cabot an annual salary of 50,000 maravedis, and gave him permission to go and fetch his wife and family from England.   No objection was raised there. The English thought very little of the new lands.   The expeditions thither had not been profitable.   No gold had been found, nor had the rich spice regions of Cathay been reached. Three savages, clothed in skins, seem to have been the only returns made—certainly the only returns recorded.   There was no market for English manufactures with such people as these.   The English of Bristol had already a good, steady trade with Iceland, and from thence all the codfish they needed could be procured.   Why go further to a distant and unknown country, where no goods could be sold ?   So Sebastian Cabot may depart whither he may choose, with his wife, and his family, and his maps, and his theory of the sphere, and his knowledge of Baccalaos.   The English merchants will follow the lines of practical common sense business ; and the king will continue to fortify the south coast, and to wage war with France, and has no time for remote and unprofitable enterprises.

It may well be supposed that Cabot felt himself under no obligation to England.   The king of Spain had received him with great kindness, and had given him a large salary and a distinguished position.   He would have been more than human if no trace of resentment rankled in his heart.   For he was not, in truth, English-born, and had no patriotic obligation to guard English interests.   Therefore, when he was made grand pilot of Spain and head of the department of cartography at Seville, he quietly acquiesced in the suppression on the maps he supervised of all traces of his father's voyage and his father's discoveries for England.   These were known to De Ayala and reported in his despatch to Spain.   They were known to La Cosa, and they were known to Robert Thorne, as shown by his letters from Seville to the English ambassador and to king Henry VIII., and were indicated on his sketch map ; but upon the Spanish maps, made under Cabot's supervision, they were either ignored or thrust (as on Ribero's map) far away north to Greenland.   The Pope had divided these unknown lands between Spain and Portugal, and these powers considered all other nations as interlopers.   Cabot was well recompensed by the king of Spain for the use of that very knowledge of Baccalaos, which he, above others, possessed ; and that knowledge, underrated and even despised in England, was suppressed upon the Spanish and Portuguese maps.   That is the answer to Harrisse's question,[6] "Why, if Cabot's landfall had been really at Cape Breton in Baccalaos, did he not record it upon the maps he supervised while grand pilot of Spain?"

No doubt there was a want of candour in this course; but candour was not a virtue in those days, especially not in an Italian of the Renaissance which Cabot was to the very core. Mr. Nicholls, the city librarian of Bristol (appendix G), has written a book exalting him as a paragon of all virtue and knowledge. He pictures him, as in after years, "homesick for his native England"—as "flying from the tyranny, cruelty and superstition of Spain into the light of freedom and the gospel"; and he triumphantly points to the instructions drawn up for the northeast expedition, in which Cabot enjoins the daily reading of the Bible to the crew, as a proof of his evangelical zeal. But Cabot was of the colour of the rock he sat upon, and Edward VI. was then reigning. In the service of the Grand Turk he would have enjoined the reading of the Koran. While he was in the service of Spain—in the receipt of great emoluments and high honours, he stealthily intrigued with Venice to sell to that state the secret he claimed to possess of a short route to Cathay, and he justified his course to the Venetian ambassador by stating that he was Venetian born, and that his conscience smote him for not doing something on behalf of his native country. This intrigue came to naught; but when, in his old age, he went to England, he renewed it while he was an English official and in receipt of English pay. At the same time he was maintaining in England that he was English, and born in the city of Bristol. So he told Richard Eden, and so it is set down in many English books. If, therefore, the map of 1544 were the only evidence of the landfall at Cape Breton, it would not, supposing it even to be Cabot's work, be entitled to more acceptance than his maps while grand pilot of Spain. Biddle, in his "Memoir of Sebastian Cabot" (appendix G), had gone very far in suppressing the father in the interest of the son; but the Bristol librarian, in what d'Avezac[a] rightly calls "parish patriotism" (*patriotisme du clocher*), after mourning over what he fondly thinks was Cabot's only lie, exhausts the language of approval by calling him the "founder of England's mercantile marine"; "the man who gave to England the carrying trade of the world" and he caps the climax of eulogy by calling him "the father of free trade." Henry Stevens, in his characteristic style, vindicates John Cabot's reputation in the formula "Sebastian Cabot—John Cabot = Zero," and, of late years, the discovery of fresh documents has re-established the merit of the elder Cabot. The balance is even inclining the other way; for Mr. Harrisse, in his last book, would seem to maintain that Sebastian Cabot was little more than a pretender to nautical knowledge. This is hard to believe, because Ferdinand and Charles V. were good judges of men, and they trusted him to the last. Indeed, when in 1547, he, without the knowledge or consent of the emperor, transferred his services to England, his salary was running on; and he drew it, when in England, as long as Charles V. would pay it, although he had no intention of going back to Spain, and with excellent judgment had declined all requests to return to his official duties there.

While Sebastian Cabot was thus sitting as grand pilot at the centre of Spanish cartography, the French and Portuguese and Basques were diligently opening up the fisheries of Baccalaos and following the whales down the Labrador coast through the straits of Belle-Isle and into the Grand bay. All this Cabot must have known, but on the Spanish maps he certified it was ignored. The first indication of a knowledge of the gulf appeared, as has been already shown, on the Portuguese maps in the same year that Jacques Cartier sailed into it from the north. The second voyage of Cartier revealed to the world the gulf and river in their full extent up to Hochelaga. It is true that the narrative of his voyages was not printed until 1545; but the Dieppe school of cartographers had commenced their labours of making known the achievements of French mariners while preparing charts to assist them in their further ventures; and on Rotz' map and the mappemonde Harleyenne in 1542, the main features of Cartier's voyages were given. Whoever compiled the map of 1544 had abundance of material in the French and Portuguese maps, as for the Spanish maps they had been far in arrears; but in 1537 the *Padron Real*, or royal standard map, as before stated was revised by a commission, and from the description given by Oviedo of its main features, it is clear that the map of 1544 was not based upon it, and was therefore not of Spanish origin, and not by Sebastian Cabot, the grand pilot of Spain.

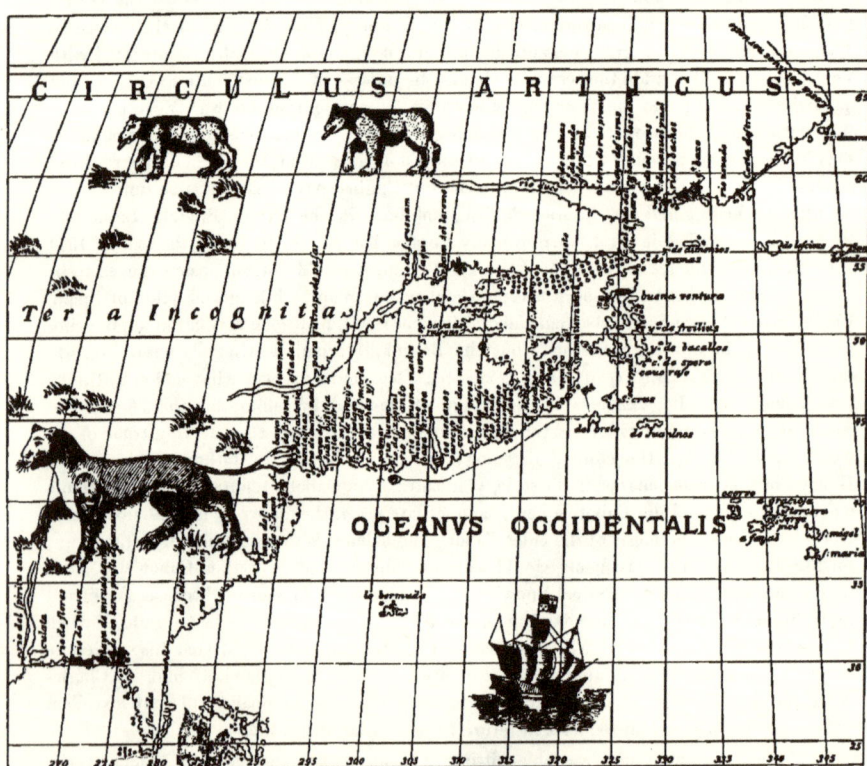

The North American Portion of the (Cabot ?) Mappemonde of 1544.

The map now under discussion, the celebrated map of 1544 (so called) of Cabot, has been described by Dr. Bourinot in his history of Cape Breton, where also the sketch here reproduced of the North American part of it may be found. It is unique, only one copy being known to exist, and was secured for the National Library of Paris. It was found in the year 1843 by Von Martius in the house of a Bavarian curate. It is engraved on copper;

but on the sides are descriptive legends in letter press, divided into two tables numbered one and two and attached after the plate was struck off. There can be no doubt but that the legends form part of the original publication, because upon the map proper are numbered references which identify them with it. There are twenty-two legends, seventeen of which are in two languages, Latin with a Spanish translation, and five in Spanish alone.

Although reproductions of the American portion are frequent enough, the whole map (for it is a *mappemonde*, or map of the world) has not often been reproduced. It is accessible to us in the facsimile in Jomard's "Monuments de la Géographie." It professes to embody all discoveries down to the date of its publication, and to that end gathers materials from all sources, even as far back as Pliny's Natural History.

In 1544 Cabot had got through the law-suits and troubles consequent upon the unfortunate expedition to the Rio de la Plata and had been restored to his high position; still the map was not published in Spain. It bears no publisher's name nor place of publication. The map, when it mentions Cabot, speaks in the third person, thus: "Sebastian Cabot made this figure"; "the said Sebastian Cabot, my author"; "discovered by John Cabot and himself;" "that most honest man, John Cabot, and his son;" "my author, the most learned of all in knowledge of astronomy and navigation"; but in the 16th legend the compiler speaks in the first person, "How Ptolemy places it (Trapovana) is, I think, known to all"; and, in the Latin version of the legend No. 17, the relation of Cabot is more precisely stated; not, as in the Spanish, "made this figure," but "laid the last touch to me (the map)," thus modifying very much the force of the argument founded on the Spanish version alone.

The geographical basis of the map is Portuguese, upon which is grafted information from French sources. Most of Cartier's names are given, as well as the results of his second voyage, thus demonstrating the existence of charts made by Cartier to which the compiler had access, and, although the names are much corrupted in translation and transcription, they can be, for the most part, identified by a reference to other charts of about that date and later.

The map appears to be the work of some very careless person, and the proofs could never have been corrected by such a man as Cabot. The Latin of the legends is rough and incorrect, as *corvi* for *cervi*. The Spanish inscriptions are admitted to be ungrammatical, and could not have passed a Spaniard; nor would it have been necessary in the legends for Cabot to explain to Spaniards that "Seville was a famous city of Andalusia." Still it must have been published in some part of the dominions of Charles V., and Winsor is probably correct in supposing Antwerp to be the place. The editing is careless; for instance, the reference in the body of the map to the legend No. 8, concerning Baccalaos, is given as No. 3; on the right hand margin of the map the latitude reads 90 degrees instead of 80 degrees;[64] the year 1494 is given instead of 1497. The Latin version of the legend No. 8 gives July 24 as the date of the landfall, while the Spanish version gives the correct date, June 24; the reference to Pliny at No. 18 cites the wrong chapter; at the Orcades there is a reference to a legend No. 30, whereas there are only twenty-two legends in all; the spelling is inconsistent and is twisted so as to be inaccurate in any language; Lake St. Peter, called Lac d'Angoulême, is, of course, translated into Spanish, but it is spelled *Laaga de Golesme*, and, just underneath, on the lake is a place called *Golosme*, as if there were some town there of that name—this same error is found on Homem's map, which is undoubtedly

Portuguese; the town or station called Brest, on Old Fort Bay, is given twice on the Labrador coast; *Cap Tiennot* is twisted into *de tronot*, while in another place is laid down *y' de tronot*. The Saguenay river is given as *R. de S. quenain*, and near it is another evident double, *Saqui*. Then there are unmeaning names, such as *tuttonaer*, on the River St. Lawrence above Lake St. Peter; this is evidently a corruption of some French name on Cartier's charts; probably *tuttonaer estndas* means " Country of the Tudemans[81]' " of Cartier. Baie de S. Laurent becomes *baya de S. loreme*. Cartier's Baie de S. Lunaire is *C. del maro*. These errors and corruptions would imply a compilation of material by an unskilful hand from all the authors then extant. I have confined my remarks to errors in the Canadian names only. Kohl and Harrisse point out many others elsewhere.

There is also another class of errors; *e. g.*, Ireland is drawn too large, as being almost equal to England and Scotland combined; in England, Dover and Yarmouth are laid down, but not Bristol, the second city of the kingdom, and the place from whence both the Cabot expeditions sailed, and, moreover, which Cabot, when in an English mood, claimed as his birthplace. All the Labrador coast is fringed with conventional islands in rows exactly four deep; Newfoundland is broken up into many detached islands—that is not remarkable, for many later maps do the same; but in this map little conventional islands are strung all through the interstices. All the islands on the coast are laid down in the most symbolic way, as if from some narrative which simply stated that the coast was studded with many islands.

The information contained in the legends is collected from all treatises on cosmography, ancient and modern, and represents the current popular belief of the time. But many of them contain stories of fabulous monsters which Cabot must have been too well informed to believe. Men with pigs' heads, who cannot talk but only grunt—of these monsters not only descriptions on the margin but drawings are given upon the map itself. Then there are people with ears so large as to cover their bodies, and men without joints in their knees or feet; there are men who whistle their communications to each other but cannot speak; there are birds which pick up an ox or a ship; there are lampreys which attack ships. These last might be gigantic octopods; but when it is related, on the authority of Pliny, that there is a fish called the *echinis* or *remora*, only half a foot long, which can stop a ship under full sail, and when a drawing of this wonderful creature is given, it becomes clear that such matter could never have been revised by Cabot. Yet whoever compiled this map must have had some communication, direct or indirect, with Cabot; because there are some particulars noted in legends Nos. 8 and 17, about the first voyage to America and the variation of the compass, which would seem to have come from him; but even they are stated obliquely in the third person, as if the map were itself speaking. The theory which seems most plausible is a modification of Mr. Harrisse's latest view. It is that Cabot was at that time meditating a transfer of his services to England. The negotiations must have been secret, since in 1545 Cabot, with Gutierez and Alonzo de Chaves, was appointed on a commission to examine De Medina's *Arte de Navegar*. That is the last record of him in Spain. Suddenly, in 1547, an entry in the minutes of council of King Edward VI. to pay the expenses of his removal, shows his presence in England. Cabot covered his hand so successfully in his intrigues with Venice in 1523 and 1551 that it was only during very recent researches in the Venetian archives that his methods came to light. As pilot major of Spain he would not dare either to publish in Spain or to contribute to the publication elsewhere of information from the Spanish official documents, it was that which caused the deprivation of Diego Gutierez the younger; but he would not be indisposed to communicate information concerning himself to a third party for use by this anonymous compiler, the more especially as publication was to be made at a distance from Spain and near to England. It was characteristic of his oblique methods, for he could not be held responsible for such a publication. The map was based on Portuguese and French documents; and, as pointed out above, he could not have seen the proofs; but still upon the map appeared information bearing on his English plans. The name of John Cabot alone stood in the English archives, to the knowledge and within the memory of many then living, as the discoverer of the new found land over the Atlantic. Sebastian could have no status in England save in so far as he could associate his name with that of John Cabot; therefore the elder Cabot after a suppression of forty years, was suddenly resurrected as the discoverer of America, precisely at the juncture when it became the interest of his son that such should be the case.

It is abundantly evident that there were at the end of the century many maps ascribed to Cabot extant, and it is also beyond question (appendix II) that they were not alike. They differed in the date of publication, some being dated 1544, two years before Cabot left Spain; some dated 1549, two years after he settled in England. A comparison of the legends is made in appendix II; but it would appear evident from Purchas that the map referred to by Hakluyt in the queen's gallery as having been cut by Clement Adams, was dated 1549. Copies of this map were in the merchants' houses,[69] and that version of the map might well be supposed to have Cabot's approval, so far as that was of value. Referring to appendix II a number of interesting questions which would be confusing here, it would be well to concentrate attention upon the inquiry whether there is any clue to indicate the features of that map which Adams engraved and Hakluyt saw. It would appear that such a clue exists.

Whatever information Clement Adams's map contained must have been common information in Hakluyt's time; because it is expressly recorded that the map was in "many ancient merchants' houses." The reason for supposing the landfall of 1497 to have been at Cape Breton east point have been given, and rests upon other foundations; but if the island of St. John had been our Prince Edward island, all the merchants would have known that fact, and it would have come out in some of the many narratives given in Hakluyt—but no mention is made of any such island in the gulf.

Again, all the merchants knew (and Hakluyt records some of their ventures in that direction) of the island of Ramea in the gulf. That island was much frequented, and is mentioned in many places in Hakluyt. It is identified as the great Magdalen, not only by its physical features, but by its attendant islands—the two Birds and Bryon island. The island of Ramea lies across the path of vessels sailing through the strait at St. Paul, and no other island is met or laid down until Anticosti is reached. The island in the Paris map is identified as Ramea, or the great Magdalen; first, by its position in the track of vessels sailing through the strait, and second, by the three little islets at the northeastern extremity, which are Bryon island and the two Bird islands, and by a little island at the other extremity which is Deadman's island—the Alezay of Cartier. The thickened form of the island betrays the Portuguese origin of the map, for the same shape is given in Vallard's and Homem's maps; while on the Dauphin map, which is wholly French, the same position is occupied by an island of the correct shape of the great Magdalen.

Again, it has been shown by Ganong and Pope that the only islands discovered by Cartier, as islands, were (what were afterwards called) the great Magdalen and its satellites. These must, therefore, first be found upon any map before we can commence to look for Prince Edward island; but, when the Magdalen group is abstracted, no other island is left, either on Cabot's or on any other map, until Champlain's large map of 1632.

Again, Michael Lok's map of 1582, in Hakluyt's "Divers Voyages," illustrates the

Michael Lok's Map, A.D. 1582.

same thesis. It is given as based on Verrazano's map, but the information current at the time is added, for Hochelaga and Saguenay are laid down, and, what is beyond question, the great Magdalen (or Ramea) is shown in its proper place. This map reveals the information current among merchants. It must be held to indicate in a general way the features of the gulf as laid down on the map of Clement Adams which Hakluyt saw. Upon it at Cape Breton is marked J. Gabot, 1497, and off Cape Breton is marked the island of St. John, near where it has been shown to have been on the long series of maps we have been following.

Again—in a few copies (twelve in all) of the second edition of Hakluyt's "Principal Navigations," published 1598–1600—in three volumes folio, is a map celebrated by having been identified as the map alluded to by Shakespeare (Twelfth Night, Act III., Sc. 2) as the "new map with the augmentation of the Indies." This map bears the following inscription upon the northern part of Labrador (near an opening in the continent marked "a furious overfall," intended for Hudson's strait) : "This land was discovered by John and Sebastian "Cabot for King Henry VII., 1497." In this respect the map favours the theory of a landfall far north at Labrador by the two Cabots in 1497, and not in 1498, thus contradicting Lok's map, which places the landfall at Cape Breton by the inscription there, "John Gabot, 1497." The question of the landfall of the first voyage has been argued in the first

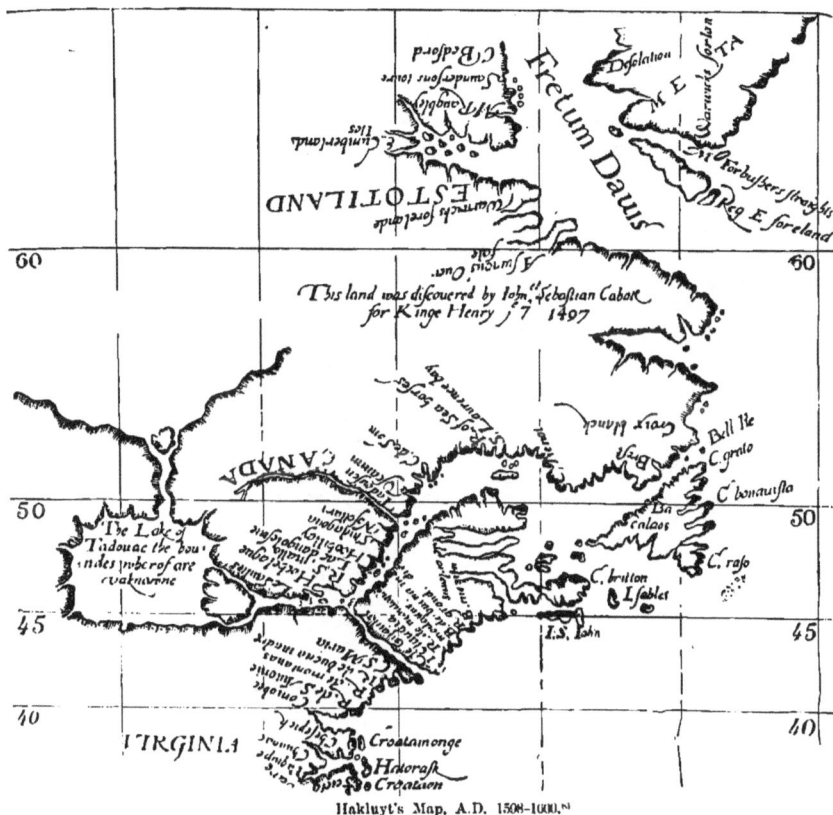

Hakluyt's Map, A.D. 1508–1600.

part of this paper on other grounds, and Hakluyt in his translation of Galvano gives it at 45°,
but this map is conclusive as to the position of the island of St. John, for it is placed in the
Atlantic, on the coast of Cape Breton and south of the east cape. An island in the gulf is
given, but its position and its shape, concave with attendant islets, mark it unmistakably as
the island of Ramea (Magdalen), so frequently mentioned in the text of Hakluyt's work,
while the deep indentations of the Nova Scotia coast show the commencement of the
separation of Prince Edward island from the mainland.

Lastly—Lescarbot's map in his history of New France demonstrates the truth of the
preceding argument. He was in Nova Scotia with Champlain, and retained his interest in
the country after his return to France. His map was published in 1609, and he shows
beyond all doubt the island of Prince Edward still adherent, but commencing to detach itself from Nova Scotia. The water is creeping inwards east and west in deep bays, but the
passage through Northumberland strait is still blocked; and, out in the gulf, in their
places and named with Cartier's names, are the islands of the Magdalen group.

I have not considered it necessary to prove that if Cabot's landfall were Cape North he could not have discovered the low-lying shore of Prince Edward island on the same day. I have preferred to show that Prince Edward island was not known as an island and did not appear on any map for one hundred years after John Cabot's death. If Cabot had possessed a modern map, and had been looking for Prince Edward island, and had pushed on without landing at the north cape of Cape Breton, and had shaped his course southward, he might have seen it in a long midsummer day ; but Cabot did not press on. He landed and examined the country, and found close to it St. John's island, which he also examined. Upon that easternmost point of this Nova Scotian land of our common country John Cabot planted the banner of St. George on June 24, 1497, more than one year before Columbus set foot upon the main continent of America, and now, after almost four hundred years, despite all the chances and changes of this western world, that banner is floating there, a witness to our existing union with our distant mother land across the ocean. May the *cavo descubierto por Ingleses* ever be thus adorned ; and, meantime, when in 1897 St. John the Baptist's day arrives, what shall Canadians do to commemorate the fourth centenary of that auspicious day when the red cross was planted on the mainland across the western sea, and when on a point of land in our own Dominion the English tongue was heard, of all the languages of Europe the first, upon this great continent—from the desolate shores of the Arctic ocean on the north to the silent wastes of the Antarctic on the south ?

APPENDIX A.

Champlain's explanation of two maps of New France in his " Voyages " (1613) at p. 413 of the edition edited by the Abbé Laverdière.

" I have thought proper to say a few words, also, touching the two maps, so as to make them understood ; for though one is the counterpart of the other so far as ports, bays, capes, headlands and rivers running inland are concerned, they differ as to the situations. The small one is in its true meridian, according to the method demonstrated by Sieur de Castelfranc in his book on the ' Mécométrie of the Magnetic Needle,' wherein I have remarked several declinations which have been most useful to me, as will be seen by the said map, with all the altitudes, latitudes and longitudes, from the forty-first to the fifty-first degree of latitude towards the north pole, which are the limits of Canada as far as the Grand bay, in which the Basques and Spaniards generally carry on their whale fishery. I have also noticed at certain places in the great river St. Lawrence, at the forty-fifth degree of latitude, as much as twenty-one degrees of variation of the magnetic needle, which is the greatest that I have seen. The small map may well be used in navigating, provided one knows how to set the needle to the compass card. For example, to use it, it is necessary, for greater facility, to take a compass card whereon the thirty-two points are equally marked, and fix the point of the magnetic needle at 12, 15 or 16 degrees from the fleur-de-lis on the northwest side, which is nearly a point and

Part of Champlain's small map in its true meridian.

a half ; that is, one point from the northwest towards the north, or a little more than a point from the fleur-de-lis of the card, and place the card in the compass on arriving at the Grand bank where the fishery is carried on. By this means one can find with certainty all the altitudes of the capes, ports and rivers. I know that a great many will not use the small map, and will rather resort to the large map, more especially as it is based on the compass of France, where the magnetic needle points northeast, because they are so well accustomed to that method that it is difficult to induce them to do otherwise. On this account I have prepared the large map in that way, for the benefit of the majority of pilots and navigators to New France, fearing that if I had not done so I would have been charged with a fault they could not account for, because the small charts or maps of the new lands mostly disagree as to the situations and altitudes of the coasts, and if there are a few who possess some small maps which are pretty correct, they consider them so valuable that they do not make them publicly known so as to put them to good use. Map making is done in such a way that north-northeast is taken as the meridian line, and west-northwest as west. It is contrary to the true meridian of this place to call north-northeast the north ; because instead of the needle being taken to point to the northwest, it is taken as pointing to northeast, as if it were in France. The error has therefore continued and will continue, for they cling to their old customs, though it leads to grave errors. A compass set north and south is also in use,[13] in which the point of the magnetic needle is fixed right under the fleur-de-lis. A good many prepare their small maps according to this compass, which seems to me to be the best, and to approach nearer to the true meridian of New France than the compasses of Eastern France set to northeast. Thus it happened that the early navigators who sailed to parts of New France in the west, thought they would not be more astray in going thither than when going to the Azores, or other places near France, where the variation is almost insensible in navigation, and where the pilots have no other compasses than those of France set to north-east, and representing the true meridian there. And so, when sailing continually towards the west and wishing to keep on a certain latitude, they would shape their course straight towards the west by their compass, thinking they were sailing on the parallel they wished to go upon.[14] But continuing on in a straight line, and not in a circle, like all parallel lines on the globe, after a long distance when in sight of land, they sometimes found themselves three, four or five degrees more southerly than necessary, and thus they were deceived in their latitude and reckoning. It is very true, however, that with fine weather and the sun shining, they would correct their latitude, but it was not without wondering why the course was wrong, which was, because instead of sailing in a circular line according to the parallel, they ran in a straight line, and, thus, as the meridian changed the points of the compass changed, and consequently the course. It is then most necessary to know the meridian and the variation of the magnetic needle, and it is of service for all pilots sailing round the world, and specially at the north and south, where the greatest variations of the magnetic needle occur, and also where the circles of longitude are smaller, since their error would then be greater

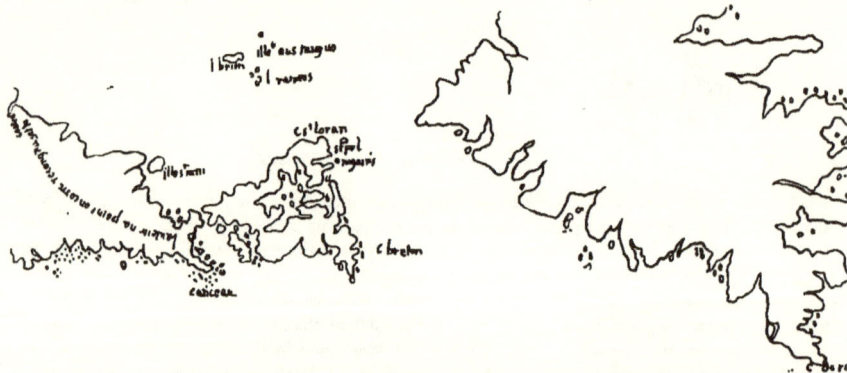

Part of Champlain's large map (1612) drawn to the compass of Eastern France.

if they did not know the variation of the magnetic needle. The error then having thus originated, and sailors being unwilling, or not knowing how, to correct it, it has remained as it is to this day, so that it is difficult to alter this system of navigating in these parts of New France. This is why I have prepared this large map, both on account of its being more full than the small one, and because it will be more satisfactory to sailors, who will be able to sail by it in the same manner as by their small charts. They must forgive me if I have not made the maps better or more in detail, as the lifetime of a man would hardly suffice to learn anything so thoroughly but in time he will find something omitted. Observant persons of an inquiring mind will see during their travels things that are not set down on this map, and they can insert them, so that in the course of time doubts will be cleared up about such matters. I think that I have done my duty as far as I could, for I have forgotten nothing that I have seen worthy to be put on my said map, and I have given clear information to the public concerning things which had never before been described or discovered so exactly, for although in years past some one may have written about them, it was trifling in comparison with what we have discovered in the last ten years." [74]

CHAMPLAIN'S NOTES ON THIS MAP.

"I have made this map for the convenience of the majority of those who sail on these coasts, for many use compasses set for the hemisphere of Asia, by which they navigate. If I had made this map like the small one, most sailors would have been unable to use it, through being unacquainted with the variations of the needle."

"Note that on this map north-northeast stands for north, and west-northwest for west; this will help you to get the elevations of the degrees of latitude as if it were the true east and west and north and south; inasmuch as the said map is made on the compass of France set to northeast."

APPENDIX B.

VARIATION OF THE COMPASS.

The fact of the variation of the compass having once been observed it occurred to Columbus to use it as a means of determining longitudes at sea. In those days dead reckoning was the only method known and, while the latitudes of old maps are fairly correct, the longitudes are far, often absurdly far, astray. The log line was not used until after Magellan's voyage in A.D. 1521, and the speed of sailing was estimated by the eye with the aid of a half-hour sand-glass. In his second voyage, Columbus attempted to put to practical use his observations upon the variation of the needle, and Sebastian Cabot was all his lifetime haunted by a similar idea. He is erroneously supposed by many to have first observed the variation and he seems to have claimed it (see p. 64). Livio Sanuto (Geografia Distinta, Venice, 1588) states that he was informed by Sebastian Cabot that the point of no variation was 110 miles to the westward of the meridian of Flores. The latitude is not recorded but it was probably 46° north. Cabot told the Venetian ambassador to Spain (Contarini) that he alone knew of a way to determine longitude by variation. The same idea is met in Champlain's voyages, and, in the "Arcano del Mare," a method is proposed for the purpose. The line of demarcation drawn by the bull of Alexander VI. was a meridian 100 leagues west of the Azores, and the idea that the needle changed to the west at that point had an influence in fixing the line, but not long after, by the treaty of Tordesillas, the line was, for other reasons, moved to a meridian 370 leagues west of the Cape de Verde islands. Longitude was for a long time calculated from Pico, an island in the Azores 28° 28' west from Greenwich. Captain John Davis (in his "Seamen's Secrets," London, 1607,) says that longitude was calculated from St. Michael's, one of the Azores as the meridian of no variation, and English sailors continued to reckon from that point until the establishment of Greenwich observatory. On the latest charts the point of no variation is at 24° west.

Ruysch, who made the map in the Ptolemy of 1508, (see p. 76) the first engraved map showing America, sailed on one of the earliest voyages to the northeast coast of the new world. He was probably on the second Cabot voyage, and a note upon his map indicates some extraordinary experience on the north of Labrador. "Here a raging sea begins;here the compasses of the ships do not retain "their properties and ships having iron are not able to return." He must have been near the magnetic pole of that era. [71] The great problem among sailors and maritime nations then and for two hundred years later was to find a method of determining longitude. Large standing rewards were instituted by Philip II. and by the state of Holland for the discovery of that secret.

APPENDIX C.

FABYAN'S CHRONICLE.

In the Chronicles of England, by John Stow, published in 1580, the following passage occurs at p. 862, as extracted from the Chronicle of Robert Fabyan:—

"In Anno 14, Henr. VII."—(Aug. 22, 1498, to Aug. 21, 1499.)

" This yeare, *one Sebastian Gabato, a genoa's sonne borne in Bristow* professing himself to be
" experte in knowledge of the circute of the worlde and Ilandes of the same, as by his Chartes and
" other reasonable demonstrations he shewed, caused the King to man and victual a shippe at Bristow
" to search for an Ilande which he knewe to be replenished with rich commodities; in the ship
" diverse merchauntes of London adventured smal stockes, and in the company of this shippe, sayled
" also out of Bristow three or foure smal shippes fraught with slight and grosse wares as course cloth
" caps, laces, points and such other " * * * *

Harrisse conjectures with the greatest probability that Stow meant the current year 1498 and not strictly the regnal year. The voyage then falls in with the letters patent of 1498 and the date agrees with the following citation which purports to be also extracted from the same work.

FROM HAKLUYT'S "DIVERS VOYAGES," PUBLISHED 1582.

" A note of Sebastian Gabote's Voyage of Discoverie, taken out of an Old Chronicle, written by
" Robert Fabian, sometime Alderman of London, which is in the custodie of John Stow, Citizen, a
" diligent searcher and preserver of Antiquities.
" In the 13 yere of King Henrie the VII., 1498." (Aug. 22, 1497, to Aug. 21, 1498.)
" This yere the King (*by means of a Venetian*, whiche made himself very experte and cunning in
" knowledge of the circuit of the worlde, and Ilandes of the same as by a Carde, and other demonstra-
" tions reasonable hee shewed), caused to man and victuall a shippe at Bristowe to search for an
" Ilande, whiche hee saide hee knewe well was riche, and replenished with riche commodities.
" Which ship, thus manned and victualed at the Kinge's cost divers merchants of London ventured
" in her small stockes, *being in her, as chief Patrone, the saide Venetian*. And in the companie of the
" saide shippe sayled also out of Bristowe, three or foure small ships, fraught with sleight and grosse
" merchandizes, as course cloth, Caps, Laces, points and other trifles, *and so departed from Bristowe in*
" *the beginning of May ; of whom in this Maior's time returned no tidings.*"

The mayor of London was William Purchas and his time expired on October 28th, 1498. At that date then the expedition had not returned. The words in the extracts printed in italics differ in the two versions. Hakluyt and Stow were quoting from what would appear to be a MS. chronicle in the possession of the latter. Hakluyt's extract says the padrone or commander was a Venetian. In his prefatory note he calls him Sebastian Cabot. Stow says in his extract that he was Sebastian Cabot the son of a Genoese and born in Bristol. John Cabot was in fact born in Genoa but a subject of Venice. Each writer seems to have taken from the MS. what struck his attention.

Hakluyt in his *Principal Navigations* published in 1600, (vol. 12, p. 31, Goldsmith's ed.) repeats the quotation from Fabyan but, in the intervening eighteen years, he would seem to have made further researches while preparing his great work. He now inserts the name in the extract—" One *John Cabot*, a Venetian, who made, etc.," but, as if to perplex future historians, he changes the prefatory note only very slightly to "a note of Sebastian Cabot's first discovery taken out of *the latter part* of Fabian's Chronicle."

The perplexing part of this question is that Fabyan's Chronicle was printed and published in 1516, in 1533, in 1542, and in 1559, (see Lowndes) before Hakluyt and Stow wrote, and in none of these editions is there the slightest notice of the Cabots or their voyages. Harrisse has found in the British Museum a MS. chronicle from which he quotes in his "Jean et Sébastien Cabot." He thinks it is a copy of Fabyan, but Winsor (Narr. & Crit. Hist.) denies that it is a Fabyan and says that there is in the museum a genuine MS. Fabyan but it also says not one word of Cabot.

Harrisse's MS. is as follows :—

"In Anno 13, Henry VII,"—(Aug. 22, 1497, to Aug. 21, 1498.)

" This yere the king at the besy request and supplicacion of a *Straunger venisian,* which by a " Cœnrt made hym self expert in knowyng of the world caused the Kyng to manne a ship w^t vytaill " and other necessaries for to seche an Ilande wheryn the *said Straunger* surmysed to be grete com- " modities: w^t which ship by the Kynge's grace so Rygged went 3 or 4 moo owte of Bristowe, *the* " *said Straunger beying Conditor of the saide Flete,* wheryn dyuers Merchaunts *as well of London* as " Bristow adventured goodes and sleight Merchandises, which departed from the West Cuntrey in the " begynning of Somer *but to this present moneth came never Knowlege of their exployts.*"

The substance of all these extracts is the same, and they in no way affect the conclusions of this paper. The "Patrone," the "Conditor" of the fleet is the "Venetian," the "Stranger Venetian," which indicates that John Cabot sailed in command on the voyage of 1498. Sebastian's name is put forward by Hakluyt in 1582, but withdrawn in 1600. In Stow's version in 1580 there is no indication of any other. This would show that he sailed on the voyage and that in 1580, twenty-three years after his death, the memory of the elder Cabot, who died in 1498, eighty-two years before, had well nigh faded out, and that it is only when Hakluyt made his researches for his great work that he came upon documents—perhaps the letters patent—which revealed the name of the chief discoverer. All the extracts will be seen to refer to the same, viz., to the second voyage.

APPENDIX D.

Estevan Gomez.

The voyage of Gomez was made in 1525 in one small vessel and occupied ten months. He appears to have been in search of an opening into the great southern ocean. When Alonzo de Chaves revised the official chart of Spain in 1536 he availed himself of the information brought back by Gomez, and no doubt Gomez himself made a chart and wrote an account of his voyage, but all these documents have been lost. Oviedo gave in 1537 a description of the coast, based upon De Chaves' revised chart which he had before him. A further summary was made by Alonzo de Santa Cruz^{xx} in his *Islario* of 1560, and Harrisse quotes largely from a manuscript *Islario* by Cespedes compiled in 1598. A very interesting discussion has been carried on for many years over those writings, into which it would be irrelevant to the present purpose to enter. Many of the localities are in dispute and Oviedo's description is far from being easy to follow; but some points are clear, and among them it should be noticed that Gomez most certainly sailed along the coast of Cape Breton. The island is mentioned by the name of the island of St. John and the strait of Canso, separating it from the mainland, under the name of the canal of St. Julian.^{xt} Passing along the coast Gomez saw columns of smoke and concluded that the country was inhabited. He reported it as well wooded with large rivers opening into the sea. The smoky cliffs of Cap Enfumé, and the openings of the Bras d'Or with the pleasant forest land around them plainly mark the locality. There are no indications, either in books or maps, that Gomez sailed into the gulf of St. Lawrence. The description extant follows along the south coast of Newfoundland to Cape Race.

Mr. Harrisse (Discovery of America, p. 237) is much exercised about this voyage, but his perplexity arises from his fixed idea that the island of St. John was a delusion of the Portuguese pilots.

Reinel's or Champlain's map or any other of the older maps drawn to a magnetic meridian will show "the bay of the Bretons" mentioned by Santa Cruz, for it is the sheet of water bounded between Cape Race and Cape Canso.

The especial facts bearing on the present inquiry are, that the island of St. John of Gomez, De Chaves, Santa Cruz, and Cespedes, is Cape Breton and not Prince Edward island, and that there are a sufficient number of islands in this "bay of the Bretons" including the 11,000 Virgins to fill the requirements of Fagundes' grant without going up to Anticosti or Crane island in the river St. Lawrence.

APPENDIX E.

JOAM ALVAREZ FAGUNDES.

The Rev. Dr. Patterson, in the 'Trans. R. Soc. Can.' for 1890, published an exhaustive paper on the movements of the Portuguese on the northeast coast of America in the early part of the sixteenth century. His account of Fagundes and of the grant made to him is as full as the records permit; for, in truth, the details are exceedingly scanty. The maps show that as early as 1505 the openings in the coast at Belle-Isle and at St. Paul's were known, and the same maps also prove that the gulf and its contents were not known until Cartier opened them up to the world. It was not by Canso or St. Paul's but by following the whales down the Labrador coast and into the Grand bay that the French and Basques entered the gulf; and Cartier pushed their enterprises to the limit of navigation at Montreal. It has been shown that Brest (on Old Fort bay) was a rendezvous and a fishing station for the French before 1534; in like manner, beyond doubt, on the Atlantic coasts of Acadia the Portuguese had similar fishing stations at the favourite resorts of their sailors. No traces remain of what Fagundes actually accomplished; the grant made to him in 1521 shows that he claimed to have discovered the land from the limits of the Spanish discoveries on the south to those of the Cortereals on the north, and, on the strength of that claim, the crown of Portugal granted him the lordship over that extent of coast. Besides this coast line, certain islands were granted, three of which were said to be in the "Bay of Auguada which is on the northeastern and southwestern coast;" evidently on a sea-coast trending in the general direction of the Atlantic coast. These islands are furthermore specified by name, viz., St. John, St. Peter, St. Ann, St. Anthony, St. Pantaleone, and the archipelago of the 11,000 Virgins. To locate one locates them all. Besides these, the grant mentions the island of the Holy Cross and another island also, called St. Ann,[72] which had been seen but not landed upon.

Of these islands, St. John is well known and also the archipelago of the 11,000 Virgins. These last are always put down on the early maps on the south coast of Newfoundland. St. Peter is the present St. Pierre known by that name to Jacques Cartier. The island of Santa Cruz was an imaginary island which haunted the Atlantic charts far out to sea for nearly one hundred years. The archipelago of the 11,000 Virgins still clings to our charts, in name, as the Virgin rocks; their place has moved farther out upon the banks although the rocks themselves are said never to be seen but in bad weather when the breaking of the waves reveals them. St. Ann's is shown on the Harleyan map and also by Ortelius on the south coast of Newfoundland. All these islands can thus be located, and it is unnecessary to search for islands for Fagundes away up in the gulf and river St. Lawrence, as if there were no islands on the coast to which the names belong. There remain many other islands on Fagundes' coast line. There are Miquelon and Langley and Sable islands and St. Paul's and the present Ramea and numerous others on the coast. In Whytfleet's map the " Ylas Fagundez " are laid down south of Newfoundland. The testimony of the maps is unanimous that the gulf was unknown up to 1534, when Viegas gave an embryonic outline of its shape. The map of Lazaro Luis proves nothing; for it was made in 1563; or rather, it proves that Prince Edward island was not the island of St. John nor one of the islands granted to Fagundes, for its northern coast line is still seen as part of the Nova Scotia shore. As for Auguada bay Lescarbot writes that he put into the bay of Canso for water on his return home. That may, as well as any other, have been "Watering bay." It was convenient before starting on the home voyage, but water can be got anywhere where there is a harbour along the coast. The map of Lazaro Luis has an inscription along the coast of Nova Scotia to the effect that it was discovered by Gomez, "Costa que descobrio Estevan Gomez," and yet in the interior of the country is inscribed "Lavrador q descobrio Joam Alvarez," so that Fagundes would seem, if the words are taken seriously, to have discovered the interior of a continental land in 1521 of which the sea coast was not discovered until 1525, or four years later, by Stephen Gomez. The grant was of a line of coast and of islands all in the Atlantic, and Dr. Patterson's suggestion that Auguada bay was Fortune bay is most probably correct. It is impossible for any one familiar with the gulf to entertain Mr. Harrisse's opinion that Anticosti or the Magdalen or Prince Edward islands were known to Fagundes from being seen by him when sailing through the gulf to get fresh water in the St. Lawrence, nor does it seem reasonable to invoke the aid of a map dated 1563 to prove a discovery affirmed to have been made in 1521.

APPENDIX F.

THE MAGDALEN ISLANDS.

As pointed out in the main body of this paper this group of islands, as it is generally considered, ought rather to be treated as one large island after the manner of the early maps. In fact the Henry II. map of 1546 gives a fairly correct idea of the outline of the island. The description given in "The Cruise of the Alice May," p. 51, will make this clear.[76]

"The main group is practically one island; that is it consists of several islands composed of real
"soil or rocks, more or less covered with trees, connected by long stretches of sand which are broken
"at intervals by inlets. Between are shallow lagoons, generally not deep enough for a boat. Thus
"Amherst is connected with Grindstone island, and Grindstone and Alright are connected with Coffin
"island. Were it not for the inlets, one might go continuously dry-shod from Amherst to Coffin
"island. But the water in the inlets is so shoal that in places they can be forded—not, however,
"without some danger, as quicksands abound. Several detached islands lie outside of the main group.
"These are Deadman island, the Bird rocks and Bryon island."

Magdalen island then, is one large island, and a neglect of that fact has led Kohl, Da Costa, and many others to suppose that the large island in the gulf laid down on early maps is of necessity Prince Edward island, and that it is drawn out of its place. Markham in his introduction to the Hakluyt Society volume for 1893 has interpreted the maps correctly, and Ganong in 1889, 'Trans. Roy. Soc. Can.', resisted the misconception growing out of the map of 1544. These errors have obtained such currency that it is important to check them before the geographical history of the gulf is hopelessly confounded, and with this view it must be borne in mind that only one island is known in all the maps before Champlain's in 1632, and it is placed in the track of vessels sailing to the St. Lawrence river. That island is taken for Prince Edward, and the Magdalen is supposed to be omitted, while in reality it is the Magdalen which is shown and Prince Edward omitted, because this latter island is, in all the maps prior to that date, still adherent to the mainland. The sketch on the following page will make it clear that the Magdalen is the island portrayed.

Those who have sailed much in the gulf know, what the charts bear witness to, that it is impossible to pass in or out of it by St. Paul's without seeing the great Magdalen or one of its attendant islands, usually the Great Bird. Prince Edward island is never seen, not only because its shores are low and the whole island is very flat, but because it is very much out of the way of vessels (see p. 78) and, unless they steer directly for it, ships might sail in and out of the river St. Lawrence for a hundred years (as in fact they did) without suspecting its existence. Even when entering the gulf from the strait of Canso the island, if seen, would appear to be part of the mainland just as it is laid down on the maps of Rotz, Vallard, Henry II., Freire, Jomard, Homem and Lazaro Luis. The last mentioned map very clearly shows the coast line of the north shore of Prince Edward island considered as part of the mainland; and that fact alone disposes of the supposition that Fagundes saw it or that the Portuguese ever named it.` [In passing out from the strait of Canso the very bold promontory of Cape St. George for a long time closes out the open water in rear and when that is passed the more distant high lands of the Nova Scotia coast are opened up until Prince Edward island is seen; so that unless a vessel were to change its course to the southwest the existence of Northumberland strait would not be suspected, and moreover if the strait were well entered and even half sailed through Cape Tormentine and Cape Egmont overlap so as to give the appearance of a land-locked bay, and the dis_ tance between the opposite shores is at one point so small that surveys have been made for a projected tunnel to connect them. In confirmation of the late discovery of this strait the maps of Champlain may be cited. That of the voyage of 1611 lays down the Magdalens under the singular name of Isles aux gros yeux—an error of the engraver for Isles aux margaux—but no hint is given of Prince Edward island. On the larger map of 1613 appears (see p. 94) a small island with an illegible name, evidently the western section of it nearest the New Brunswick coast, in its proper place as seen from the mainland. A note on this map explains that Champlain had not himself been upon that coast and yet he and his associates had been sailing in and out of the gulf for some years.

CONTOUR OF THE MAGDALEN ON EARLY MAPS.

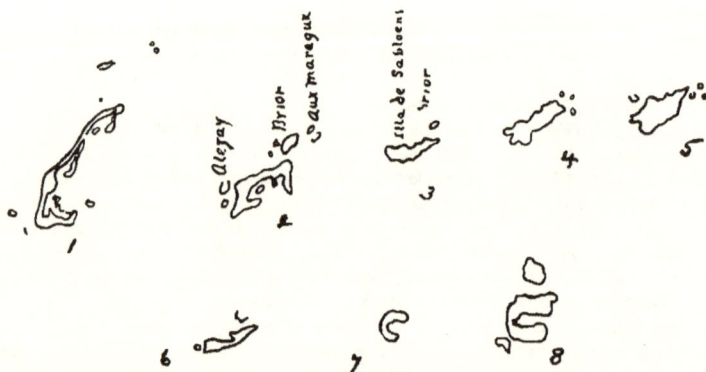

1. Magdalen island correctly drawn.

2. From the Henry II., or Dauphin, map of 1546. Alezay is Deadman's island, les Iles aux Margaux are the two Birds, and Bryon island has retained its name until now. Entry island is shown. All are in their relative places and the concave shape of Magdalen island is clearly shown.

3. From Homem's map (Portuguese) 1558. The island is identified by its name. *Ille de Sabloen*—isle of sands, and by Bryon island close to it. The concavity is turned the wrong way as in all the Portuguese maps.

4. From Mercator's map, 1569. Here it is identified by the three small islands on the north.

5. From the map of 1544. The three small islands on the north and Alezay (Deadman's island) on the west identify the Magdalen.

6. From the Vallard map of 1543. This map is Portuguese. The Magdalen is shown by Alezay on the west and Bryon on the north. The concavity is reversed as in No. 3.

7. From Rotz' globe, 1543. The author was French and embodied Cartier's discoveries on his maps. The Magdalen is indicated by its shape, concave in the right direction as in the other French map No. 2.

8. From Hakluyt's map; the scarce map of 1600. Here the shape marks out the Magdalen and Deadman's I. (Alezay) and Bryon island further identify it.

The map of 1632 has Prince Edward island laid down correctly and named Isle St. Jean. In the time of Champlain the islands were known as *les isles Ramees—or les isles Ramees-brion.* To the English the Magdalen was known under the name of the island of Ramea and under that name it is mentioned often in Hakluyt. The name Ramea has in later years been transferred to an island on the south coast of Newfoundland. We find in Hakluyt a "relation of the first voyage and discovery of the Isle Ramea in the Bonaventure 1591," and a "Voyage of the Marigold by Fisher in 1595 to the Isle

Ramon," and again, " A Voyage of Charles Leigh to the Isle of Ramea.". From these narratives it appears that the Magdalen was a place of great resort in those days by fishing craft of all the maritime nations of Europe. Some of the names in the first relation are interesting. The " Isle Duoron " shows that a Portuguese map was referred to. On Vaz Dourado's map (circa 1580) it is · " Isle Dorean ; " both are corruptions of the French " Isle d'Arènes " ; then Isle Brion is changed to " Isle Biton " and the " Isles of Aponas " recall Jacques Cartier's first voyage, when he found a large number of birds he calls apponats on the shores of one of them. The Bird rocks were those he called Isles Margaux, and on the mainland he found an immense number of birds he called *godets* and *grands apponats* of which his sailors killed more than a thousand. To this day Alright island is by the inhabitants sometimes called *isle aux Cormorants*. While these islands were thus frequented, the island of Prince Edward was not known excepting as forming part of the coast line of the present Nova Scotia. How the name " Magdalen " was first given does not anywhere appear. The supposition that Cartier gave the name is incorrect, for it is first found in Champlain's large map of 1632, and Lescarbot calls them *Isle Colombaires ou Ramées*. In 1663 the Company of New France, in conjunction with the Miscou Company, conceded these islands to François Doublet, and when he sailed to take possession his son Joan Doublet (celebrated afterwards as a corsair and as a naval officer under Louis XIV.) then not eight years old hid himself on board his father's vessel to make the voyage. Joan Doublet states in his "Journal" that his father changed the name of the largest island from Isle Brion to Isle de la Madelaine in honour of his mother. That, however, cannot be true, for the name occurs in the very concession itself, besides being found in Champlain's map. Denys also (in whose jurisdiction all these islands were) gives the name Madelaine to the large island (see map in Bourinot's Cape Breton.) Doublet's enterprise was unsuccessful and the islands were re-granted to M. de St. Pierre in 1719. Even then the names were not settled for in the grant they are styled the " Magdalen Islands, Brion or Ramées."

APPENDIX G.

Two Memoirs of Sebastian Cabot.

There are several points in the discussion of this question which could not be considered in the main portion of the present paper without overloading it with detail, and among them is the singular warmth which some writers have imported into it. Chief among the books of authority is the " Memoirs of Sebastian Cabot," by Richard Biddle, 1831. This is a work of very great research and indispensable to all students ; but it is marred by its manner which is that of a lawyer's brief for Sebastian Cabot against all persons whomsoever. It is impossible to say anything against John Cabot because so few notices of him survive, but he describes him out of his own head as an old merchant who did not go to sea ", and then ignores him. That is not surprising for the documents upon which the elder Cabot's reputation is based were found in the Spanish and Italian archives long after Mr. Biddle's death, but all the authors from whom he differs he has treated as if they were hostile witnesses in a criminal trial. Thus of " Barrow's Chronological History of Voyages " he writes sarcastically, as being " invaluable, as it not only embodies in a cheap and convenient form all the " mistakes of its predecessors but generally supplies a good deal of curious original error." If the old writers even do not record suitable facts, Mr. Biddle is equally severe; thus, Gomara, in his " General History, 1552," says of the east coast of America " Gomez visited a region which had never before him " been visited by any one though they say that it was first discovered by Sebastian Cabot." Gomara was merely repeating what was said in Spain and what the Spanish maps, authorized by Cabot as Grand Pilot bear witness of to this day, and yet Mr. Biddle adds " churlish expressions," " despicable temper." If any one was responsible for Gomara's statement it was Mr. Biddle's own hero who from 1512 to 1547 was the chief official in Spain to guarantee the correctness of the very maps which denied his discovery. The Rolls Office in London is censured for " unpardonable carelessness in letting a map become illegible," while in fact the wonder is that so many documents, even trivial entries in the records of King Henry VII., have been preserved at all, and the public records of England bear favourable comparison with those of any other nation. His book is full of sneers, and insinuations, and charges of perversions of plain meaning against every writer whose views do not harmonize with his own. Hakluyt often does not quote exactly the words of the writer he cites, and sometimes supplements the sense by information from other sources. Such was the method in an uncritical age. His work was a collection, not for critical study, but for practical information, and he recorded all he could learn. It was the first attempt to narrate the exploits of English seamen and he spared neither pains or money to do it. Mr. Biddle out of his own fancy describes him as a "sleek well-fed prebendary who would not "likely condescend to speak to a poor antiquary like Stow." Then, he himself, so severe upon others, is incessantly building facts upon hypotheses. He "supposes," continually and repeats "it is impossible " and "it is not improbable" and "it is incredible," and when enough of such material is spread he propounds a conclusion which he seems to think proved. So out of "if" and "probably" and "doubtless" he weaves a statement that Verrazano was with Rut on his voyage of 1527 and was killed by the Indians on the coast of America. Of this Buckingham Smith, with some of Biddle's causticity, says, "They who find instruction in speculative history may be gratified with a fine example by turn- " ing to the chapter in the Memoir of Cabot in which he (Verrazano) is supposed to have lost his life " in the service of England."

But one of the grossest instances of a grave charge made upon a mere hypothesis is his treatment of William Worthington. It will be remembered that Cabot had left Spain while he was a high official of the emperor Charles. He was in receipt of a salary from the English crown and was at least 83 years of age when, on the 27th May, 1557, he resigned and was reappointed conjointly with one William Worthington. At that date Philip II. was in England and Mr. Biddle, out of his own fancy, calls Worthington "that Worthington probably, a favourite of that dark hour." And then he goes on without the least basis to formulate the charge that Worthington, while an English official, sold to Philip all of Cabot's papers and maps to be taken to Spain. This is very effectively disproved by Hakluyt in his "Divers Voyages," who says that then (in 1582) they were in the possession of the Worshipful Master William Worthington, one of Her Majesty's (Queen Elizabeth's) pensioners, who was willing to have them published. Harrisse's theory is probably correct that Cabot was too old to perform his functions and Worthington was appointed to do the work and divide the salary. D'Avezac, a very high authority on the subject, suggests that Worthington was related to Cabot through his wife and the change was made in Cabot's interest by his friends. One theory is as good as another, but Philip was not so popular in England that a native born officer of the English crown would be likely to betray his country's interest for a Spaniard, and, if he did, it was not likely that Elizabeth's ministers would have continued him in his office and emoluments. It appears that Worthington had held some office under Edward VI. and that there had been a defalcation in his department. The official discharge shows that " in consideration of his services both in France and Scotland * * * " and for that the debt grew by unfaithfulness of his servant who ran away with the same," he was exonerated. This Mr. Biddle converts, out of his own imagination, into " the king with easy liberality " forgiving him a large debt on his allegation that a servant had run away with the money."

Whatever cause of complaint Mr. Biddle may give on account of unjust handling of his materials he did, in fact, contribute a great deal of valuable original matter to the subject. This, however, cannot be said of Mr. J. F. Nicholls, librarian of the city of Bristol, who, in 1869, published an apotheosis of Cabot under the following title : " The remarkable life, adventures and discoveries of " Sebastian Cabot, of Bristol, the founder of Great Britain's maritime power, discoverer of America, " and its first colonizer." Excepting in its outward appearance this book seems to be a model of everything a book ought not to be. Here is the author's idea of what the " Matthew " did in the time between June 24 and towards the end of July, in 34 days at most. " The first land made was the Cape " North, the northern extremity of Cape Breton, and the island opposite the same (not lying in front " of the land but further on) was Prince Edward island which was then named by them and long " afterward known as the isle of St. John. They skirted this island and sailed along the southern

" coast on the gulf of St. Lawrence, beyond the site on which Quebec at present stands, then returning
" by the northern shore of the 'gulf' still trending eastward they coasted to the latitude of 53° and
" then sailing by Newfoundland island, which they took to be and depict as an archipelago, they
" continued their course southward to the Chesapeake and so home. The *prima vista* then was the
" most northerly point of Cape Breton, and the point struck gave them a view at once of Nova Scotia
" and Prince Edward island."

The translation of *ex adverso* is remarkable, " not lying in front of the land but further on." The
Piagah-like view of Prince Edward island and of Nova Scotia from Cape North is peculiar to this
writer as is likewise Cabot's sailing beyond Quebec. The map called Cabot's of 1544 shows Cartier's
discoveries on the St. Lawrence as far as Lake St. Peter. One can hardly believe such to be the case, but
Mr. Nicholls writes as if he supposed that map was a map of the voyage of 1497, and represented the
discoveries of that year.

This book, in the words of D'Avezac, is an excellent example of parish patriotism, and
necessarily therefore Sebastian Cabot was born in Bristol, and John Cabot, who had not that privilege,
is, as D'Avezac says, "robbed of his glory to aggrandize that of his son." The disappearance of
Cabot's maps is more rhetorically stated than by Mr. Biddle and with more imagination of detail.
"This man had the custody of Cabot's maps by virtue of his office. Such documents would be
" secured by Philip at any price. He had put Worthington into the office " * * * " Well, the reader
" may draw his own conclusion. We accuse no one; but we have a deep suspicion that they may
" yet be found among her (Spain's) archives." Maps of Cabot's might be found there and still Wor-
hington be guiltless; for Cabot left Spain so privately that he is much more likely to have left all his
maps behind him; but, in fact Philip could not want maps from him, for from the nature of his office
in Spain all the Spanish maps were made under his sanction. Worthington could not have stolen the
map in the Queen's gallery. Gilbert speaks in the plural and calls them " maps " and many other maps
ascribed to him are spoken of (at the Earl of Bedford's and in merchants' houses) as existing in the
time of Queen Elizabeth. All these have also disappeared and yet were not sold to Philip. Having the
Spanish maps, made and issued under the authority of Cabot, as head of the department of cartography
for thirty years, Spain needed no more, so far as Cabot was concerned, to invalidate the claims of
England in America.

It has been shown, mainly from the secret archives of Spain and Italy, that John Cabot was the
real discoverer, yet Mr. Nicholls says, "Certainly Sebastian gives us no hint of his father's presence
" in either voyage; but modest, gentle and unassuming as all his life proves him to have been, speaks
" of the discovery ever in the first person and in the singular number." As a good Bristolian Mr.
Nicholls will have it Cabot was born is Bristol. Cabot no doubt said so—at times—in England ; and
others beside Mr. Nicholls think so; but the researches in the secret archives at Venice prove that in
his intrigues with the Council of Ten he stated that he was born in Venice. So he told Contarini and
so he wrote by his emissary, the Ragusan friar. The Council of Ten were in a position to know, for
in Roman Catholic countries registers of baptism are, and were, carefully kept, and he would not have
tried to deceive in a matter so easily disproved. Mr. Nicholls laments this one falsehood of Cabot's
blameless life; but after all he thinks it was venial, for he had a very narrow escape from being born
in Venice. No doubt it is hard to go through so long a life without telling one falsehood ; David and
Jacob and even Abraham made at least one slip, but the difference between them and Cabot is that he
kept it up to the last. Even when residing in the land of "religious liberty " so late as 1551, while an
official of England and in receipt of a salary from the crown, he resumed secret negotiations with the
Council of Ten at Venice to enter their service and impart to them some secrets of navigation which
he professed to have. His heart was then in Venice and the Council style him "our most faithful
Gaboto." As the matter appears to Mr. Nicholls "he pined in Spain for his native Bristol. Home-
" sickness came over him, he gave up the emoluments of office to live and die where he might have
" religious liberty. He left behind him the superstition and tyranny and cruelty of Spain for the light

" of the pure gospel." The picture is touching, but truth demands the statement that he took the emoluments so long as Spain would pay them. Upon the edifying circumstances surrounding the death-bed of Cabot the religious imagination of Mr. Nicholls dwells with tender eloquence. It is a pity that the only circumstances recorded concerning his death are those given already in this paper (p. 64) from Eden's work. Mr. Nicholls sums up his merits in one comprehensive eulogistic sentence. " He created " our navy, raised England's name high among nations, placed her credit on a solid foundation, and " made her citizens respected ; he was the father of free trade, and gave us the carrying trade of the " world ! !"

APPENDIX II.

The Map of 1544 and its Legends.

It will have appeared from the preceding pages that maps were extant in England and on the continent with which Sebastian Cabot's name was, to a greater or less extent, identified, and it will also have been seen that these maps differed among themselves.   There exists a wilderness of conflicting comment upon them, and to attempt to travel over it would be tedious and confusing. Grateful as every student must be to Winsor, and Deane, and Kohl, and Harrisse, and many other learned writers upon this much vexed question it will be well to start the inquiry, if possible, anew without attempting to discuss their views.

In order to gather to a focus all the original information extant concerning these maps a concordance of all the early notices will be useful.   They are :—

(A) The Hakluyt map ; seen by Hakluyt in the Queen's gallery.

(B) The Purchas map ; seen by Purchas in the same place. He gives its date as 1549.

(C) The DeLaet map ; referred to by DeLaet as existing in England in several copies.

(D) The Gilbert map ; seen by Sir Humphrey Gilbert in the Queen's gallery.

(E) The Bedford map ; seen by Richard Willes at the Earl of Bedford's at Cheynies.

(F) The Chytræus map : seen by Kochaff at Oxford.

(G) The Ortelius map ; in the list of 200 maps given by Ortelius at the beginning of his Atlas, probably seen by him in Belgium.

(H) The Livio Sanuto map ; probably seen in Venice.

(J) The Paris map ; the mappemonde dated 1554, called the Cabot map.

Of these maps A to F were seen in England, and G to J were seen upon the continent.   To narrow the question by gradual elimination I would first exclude the map referred to by Livio Sanuto, as his notice of it affords little information.   It is mentioned in his " Geografia Distinta in XII. libri," Venice, 1588, in connection with the variation of the compass.   He would seem to refer to legend No. 17 of the Paris map, but no date is given or any other information.

Ortelius is of more service.   The map he saw was engraved on copper and without name of publisher or place of publication.   This would indicate that it was like the Paris map.   Of 200 maps in his list, mostly engraved, none were printed in Spain and all save this bore indication of place or publisher.   It must here be noted that, although Ortelius saw this map, his own map of 1570 does not bear at the north any trace of its influence ; and also that he gives the name Juan, not to an island in the gulf as in the map of 1544, but to a small island south of Newfoundland and in the Atlantic ocean.

The preceding are continental copies ; coming now to English copies there is the Bedford map. It may be gleaned from this mention that it indicated a northwest passage.   It is spoken of as " Cabot's table which the Earle of Bedford hath at Cheynies."   The Gilbert map confirms this indication.   It was seen by Sir Humphrey Gilbert in the Queen's gallery, and is referred to in his discourse published in 1576.   He introduces a little confusion by giving the date of the landfall as June 11, and at Labrador on the north side.   This Canadians know to have been impossible at that season, as also is the statement, borrowed probably from Ramusio, that the sea was then open and Cabot might have sailed to the west. Gilbert speaks in the plural of "charts," but he could not have referred to this mappemonde of 1544 for this contains no such indications as he describes. There is no trace of Hudson's bay or any such northwest passage to Asia as Sir Humphrey was writing about. It contains no argument for his thesis.

I come now to the DeLaet map. The author gives in his work (published in Leyden in 1640) a fair map of the gulf based on Champlain's early map. He does not give any name to Prince Edward island. He speaks of Cabot's maps as existing in England and gives a French translation of the same legend as Hakluyt; indeed, probably, he merely translated from Hakluyt, only that, by a misprint, the date of the landfall is July 24th instead of June 24. It must be a misprint, for the legend he gives identifies the day as St. John the Baptist's day. The same mistake occurs in the Latin version of the Paris map, but the form of the quotation proves that DeLaet had the Hakluyt legend before him. Not much can be inferred from this reference.

Purchas is a more important witness. The map he saw was in the Queen's gallery, and was engraved by Clement Adams, and it bore date 1549. He speaks of it as a "great map," of which Sebastian Cabot "is often called the author," and adds, "this map some say was taken out of Sir "Sebastian Cabot's map by Clem. Adams 1549." The landfall on this map was 1497 not 1494, so here we have ground for concluding that Hakluyt's map was dated 1549, and was not the same as the Paris map of 1544. A difficulty must, however, be noted here that Hakluyt, in his "Discourse on Western Planting," written in 1584, in warm advocacy of the claims of the English crown to the continent of America from the Arctic circle to Florida, gives 1496 as the date of the discovery, and a few pages farther on he quotes Clement Adams as giving 1494 as the date. This "Discourse" is not in Hakluyt's collection of voyages, but is a MS. published for the first time in 1877 by the Maine Historical Society. It was in fact a letter written to advocate the plans of Sir Walter Raleigh. Hakluyt was beginning then to collect materials for his great work and, as in the case of his "Divers Voyages," the later and completed work must be taken to contain the matured results of his deliberate researches. The real date of the landfall is settled now by the contemporary documents recently discovered and unknown to him.

The Chytræus map presents some difficulty. It was seen in England and was dated 1549 like the Purchas map, but the Latin inscription (No. 8) is that of the Paris map of 1544, excepting that he corrects the date to June 24. He puts the year of the discovery as 1494, as in the Paris map, but gives it as 1594 by an evident misprint. Chytræus in his book does not reproduce the map but gives all the Latin legends of the Paris map and makes no mention of the Spanish ones. He gives also headings to the legends; differing in that respect from the Paris map which has only three headings. He also quotes from Pliny direct, and does not follow the erroneous citation of the Paris map. The conclusion would follow that the map Chytræus saw was an edition of the Paris map printed in 1549 on which some minor changes had been made.

There remain now to be compared the Paris map of 1544 and the map cited by Hakluyt in the Queen's gallery and cut by Clement Adams. These two maps differ radically. Hakluyt has preserved the text of legend No. 8. While the main tenor of the information is the same as that of the map of 1544 the wording differs. Before citing the legends it should be observed that the Latin versions must be taken as the originals of which the Spanish and English are translations; for Latin, in that day, was the general international language of cultivated people, and moreover when the legends on the 1544 map were set up there could have been no Spanish type, for the printer had not " ñ " with a *tilde* over it such as was, and is still, used in Spain, and he has doubled the letter and prints mannana and not mañana. The Spanish tongue was therefore not the vernacular of the printer. On Clement Adams's map, as indeed Hakluyt expressly states, the inscription was in Latin, and the context implies that no other language was used. Hakluyt translates it but glosses it throughout not, as Biddle suggests, of set purpose to distort his original but to elucidate it, as was the frequent practice among the early writers. Then the island was *ex adverso*, over which phrase many battles have been fought. Brevoort erroneously translates it "even with." Mr. Nicholls makes it "not lying in front of the land but further on," a translation which has the unique merit of flatly contradicting its original. Other translations there are, but the Latin version of the Paris map uses instead of *ex adverso* the synonym *oppositam* in which the idea of adjacency is necessarily implied, and *appositam* recorded by Chytræus intensifies this idea. In the Latin version on the Paris map the meaning is also clearly expressed that the inscription given is intended to apply generally to the whole region and not solely to the island. A new sentence commences—Hujus terræ incolæ. All these are indications that the Latin versions are the originals.

Latin Inscription No. 8 (Copied by the Late Dr. Deane) on Map of 1544.

Terram hanc olim nobis clausam aperuit Joannes Cabotus Venetus, nec non Sebastianus Cabotus ejus filius, anno ab orbe redempto 1494, die vero 24 Julii, (sic) hora 5 sub diluculo, quam terram primum visam appellarunt & Insulam quandam magnam ei oppositam, Insulam divi Joannis nominarunt, quippe quæ solenni die festo divi Joannis aperta fuit. Hujus terræ incolæ pellibus animalium induuntur, arcu in bello, sagittis, hastis, spiculis, clavis ligneis, & fundis utuntur: sterilis incultaque tellus fuit, leonibus, ursis albis, procerisque cervis, piscibus innumeris, lupis scilicet, salmonibus & ingentibus soleis unius ulnæ longitudine, aliisque diversis piscium generibus abundat, horum autem maxima copia est, quos vulgus Bacallios appellat; ad hæc insunt accipitres nigri corvorum similes, aquilæ, perdicesque fusco colore, aliæque diversæ volucres.

The version of Chytræus is the same as above but—24 Junii instead of Julii—1594 instead of 1494 and· appositam for oppositam.

Legend on Clement Adams's Map—From Hakluyt.

Anno Domini 1497, Joannes Cabotus Venetus, et Sebastianus illius filius eam terram fecerunt perviam, quam nullus prius adire ausus fuit, die 24 Junii, circiter horam quintam bene mane. Hanc autem appelavit Terram primum visam, credo quod ex mari in eam partem primum oculos injecerat. Nam quæ ex adverso sita est insula, eam appellavit insulam divi Joannis, hac opinor ratione, quod aperta fuit eo die qui est sacer Divo Joanni Baptistæ: Hujus incolæ pelles animalium exuviasque ferarum pro indumentis habent, easque tanti faciunt, quanti nos vestes preciosissimas. Cum bellum gerunt, utuntur arcu, sagittis, hastis, spiculis clavis ligneis et fundis. Tellus sterilis est, neque ullos fructus affert, ex quo fit, ut ursis albo colore, et corvis inusitatæ apud nos magnitudinis referta sit; piscibus abundat iisque sane magnis, quales sunt lupi marini et quos salmones vulgus appellat; soleæ autem reperiuntur tam longæ, ut ulnæ mensuram excedant. Imprimis autem magna est copia eorum piscium, quos vulgari sermone vocant Bacallaos. Gignuntur in ea insula accipitres ita nigri, ut corvorum similitudinem mirum in modum exprimant, perdices autem et aquilæ sunt nigri coloris.

Hakluyt's Translation, Ed. 1600.

(Words in italics are interpolated, or changed.)

In the yeere of our Lord 1497 John Cabot, a Venetian, and his sonne Sebastian (*with an English fleet set out from Bristoll*) discovered that land which no man before that time had attempted, on the 24 of June, about five of the clocke early in the morning. This land he called Prima Vista, that is to say, first seene, because as I suppose it was that part whereof they had the first sight from sea. That island which lieth out before the land, he called the island of St. John upon the occasion, as I thinke, because it was discovered upon the day of John the Baptist. The inhabitants of this *island* use to weare beasts' skinnes, and have them in as great estimation as we have our finest garments. In their warres they use bowes, arrowes, pikes, darts, wooddon clubs and slings. The soile is barren *in some places* and yieldeth litle fruit, but it is full of white beares, and stagges farre greater than ours. It yeeldeth plenty of fish, and these very great, as seales, and those which commonly we call salmons; there are soles also above a yard in length; but especially there is great abundance of that kinde of fish which the *savages* call Bacalaos. In the same island also there breed hauks, but they are so blacke that they are very like to ravens, as also their partridges and egles, which are in like sort blacke.

The phrases on the Adams's map " because as I suppose " and " as I think " mark unerringly that Cabot neither wrote the legend nor personally superintended the writing of it. The hand of the editor is plainly seen—not Hakluyt's hand; for, however he might have glossed the translation, he would not have written glosses in Latin, as if copied from the map, and then translated them with additional English glosses. Clement Adams beyond doubt had a map engraved, or re-engraved, or did the work himself, which, though it might have been copied from some chart or map of Cabot's, was not based upon the Paris map of 1544 now under review. This is manifest because both Willes and Gilbert saw it and used it to demonstrate the existence of an open northwest passage. Willes says: " The Gulfe " (Northwestern strait, Hakluyt) " is set at 61° to 64" latitude and " neere the 318th meridian " " continuing the same " bredth about 10 degrees west where it openeth southerly, more and more until it come to the " Tropic of Cancer and so runneth to the Mar del Zur." This very precise and definite information Willes saw portrayed upon the Bedford map. Sir Humphrey Gilbert saw the copy Hakluyt describes at the Queen's gallery and upon it were similar indications, for he uses it to reinforce his argument for an open northwest passage. Now the map of 1544 contains no such information—no such " gulfe," no such " strait ten degrees wide and widening out until it opens into the southern ocean."

It cannot be supposed that Cabot ceased to make maps on his arrival in England. It is just here where Michael Lok's map throws light upon the question (see p. 90). It is published in Hakluyt's Divers Voyages with high approbation and in illustration of the same geographical ideas which Willes and Gilbert were advocating. On Lok's map is the very strait in the very place indicated on the reported authority of Cabot's maps widening out into the great southern ocean. Lok's map is dated 1582 and contains later information than the Paris map, but he gives the landfall at Capo Breton by " J. Gabot, 1497," and lays down just opposite the land, in the Atlantic, the island of St. John. The conclusion is irresistible that we have here the main features of Clement Adams's map, and upon it rather than on the map of 1544 we find the geographical information drawn by Richard Willes and Sir Humphrey Gilbert from the Bedford map and the Hakluyt map which " were also in so many merchants' houses." On the other hand this map of 1544 has left no trace of its influence upon any other map or in any writer of that period, or any other period, until the last few years. Only one indication exists that it was ever seen in Spain and that has recently been found.

The indefatigable research of Harrisse has brought to light a MS. in the Royal Library at Madrid purporting to be an " explanation of the sailing chart of Columbus." It is by a Doctor Grajales of whom nothing else is known. It contains the account Columbus wrote of his third voyage, tables of the rising and setting of the sun and the whole of the twenty-two legends of the Paris map of 1544. This confirms the fact stated above that the legends were printed separately and pasted on the sides of the map, and it suggests that the map of 1544 was at some period in the possession of this Doctor Grajales in Puerto de Sancta Maria not far from Seville. Upon this somewhat slight foundation Harrisse builds a theory that Grajales made the map, whereas it can only show that he probably had a copy.

The conclusions to which all these considerations lead, are :—

1. That the Paris map of 1544 is not Cabot's in any sense which would make him responsible for its accuracy, that it was not published or prepared in Spain, that he never corrected the proofs but that he probably contributed in some measure to the material from which its unknown author compiled it.

2. That the map in the Queen's gallery engraved by Clement Adams was essentially different in its American geography from that of 1544 and that it was based on some of Cabot's charts made in England, and that Lok's map, taken with Gilbert's and Willes's statements, affords a useful indication as to what these charts contained.

3. That in the legends on the maps as well as in the statements recorded in Hakluyt and Eden the incidents of the voyages of 1497 are not distinguished from those of 1498, but both are given together in a general description of the whole northeastern coast.

NOTES AND REFERENCES.

1. *Harrisse—Discovery of North America*, p. 185.

2. These propositions are abundantly established, mainly on documentary evidence, by Harrisse—*Jean et Sébastien Cabot* and *Discovery of America*, and by Deane in *Hist. and Crit. History of America*, vol. III.; as well as by many other writers in books and periodicals who treat of some or all of these questions.

3. Discourse of the anonymous guest at the house of Frascator. Ramusio—*Navigazioni et Viaggi*, vol. I., fol. 374 D, 3rd ed., Venice, 1653; cited and translated by the chief writers upon this subject.

4. Those who hold that the landfall was in Newfoundland generally place it at Cape Bonavista, and the island of Baccalieu, not far off, they maintain by its name to be a further identification with the place called Baccalaos. This island would then be the island of St. John, discovered the same day. Foster has no doubt about it. *Voyages and Discoveries to the North*, London, 1786. See also Murray *Discoveries and Travels in North America*, London, 1829; and, in fact, all the older writers. Among the later writers who have held that view are Sulte, *Histoire des Canadiens;* the Right Rev. Dr. Howley, *Mag. of American History*, Oct., 1891, and it is often met with in popular works.

5. A great number of names of weight are found in favour of Labrador. Among them are Kohl, Biddle, Humboldt, Harrisse in his last work, *Discovery of America*, the Abbé Ferland and Garneau.

6. The map of 1544 had not been discovered when Biddle wrote. It had a great effect in changing the set of opinion towards Cape Breton and, by a misreading of the configuration upon the map, Cape North was taken to be the indicated landfall. Harrisse in 1882 (*Jean et Sébastien Cabot*) with more reason advocated Capo Percy; but he changed his mind ten years later in his last book, *Discovery of America*, 1892. Dr. Bourinot (*Cape Breton and its Memorials*), while he follows the general current and inclines to the opinion that Cape North was the landfall, does so on the authority of the map of 1544. He, however, alone of all the writers on the question, has hitherto recognized the strong claims of Cape Breton and the conformity of Scatari island with the required conditions. He was not examining this special question and while yielding to the current opinion his local knowledge prevented him from accepting it as proved.

I have not found Mr. Eben Horsford's arguments for Salem Neck sufficiently strong to lead me to consider his theory separately.

7. Captain Richard Whitbourne—*A Relation of the New-found-land*, etc., etc., London, 1622.

8. Champlain—*Voyages*, 1632; ed. Laverdière, p. 1312, Quebec, 1870.

9. In appendix to Kohl *Doc. History of Maine*, and in his writings generally.

10. *Transactions of Royal Society of Canada*, vol. IX., 1891.

11. It would be a small matter if this error were found only in the railway hand-books; but Doane, the Abbé Beaudoin, Brevoort, Harrisse and numerous other authors of eminence maintain this view.

12. Barrett—*History and Antiquities of Bristol ;* Markham—*Hakluyt Soc. Vol.* for 1893, p. xlv.; Letter of Raimondo di Soncino, Dec. 18, 1497.

13. Despatches from Dr. de Puebla, July 28, 1498, and Pedro de Ayala, July 25, 1498, to the Catholic sovereigns; Gomara *Historia*.

14. Letters patent for both voyages. See also Biddle, page 86.

15. Letter of Lorenzo Pasqualigo, Aug. 23, 1497.

16. Despatch of Pedro de Ayala, July 25, 1498.

17. Letter of Raimondo di Soncino to the Duke of Milan, Dec. 18, 1497.

18. Peter Martyr (1516), Dec. III. Bk. 6.

19. Gomara—*Historia* (1552).

20. Peter Martyr, Gomara, Ramusio, *passim*.

21. Letter of Lorenzo Pasqualigo, August 23, 1497.

22. Peter Martyr—*Decades.*

23. See the wording of the second letters patent.

24. This is shown by the second letters patent which are addressed to him alone; also by the petition of the Drapers' Company to the king in 1521, for which see Harrisse *Discovery of America*, appendix, where the merchants make very little of Sebastian Cabot's achievements.

25. Sebastian Cabot is not mentioned by Ayala, Puebla, Soncino, nor Pasqualigo. His name occurs only once in the original authorities, and then with the names of Lewis and Sancio, his brothers, in the first patent. This is a cardinal fact in the controversy.

26. Letter of Lorenzo Pasqualigo, Aug. 23, 1497.

27. Barrett—*History and Antiquities of Bristol* for the name of the vessel. For the size and number of the crew, Soncino, Dec. 18, 1497.

28. Champlain's *Voyages*, ed. Laverdière; see for Cape Breton, p. 279; La Héve (Lunenburg, N.S.), p. 156; Port Royal (Granville, on Annapolis river), p. 167; Petit Passage (Long island, St. Mary's bay, Digby), p. 162; Kennebec (Maine), p. 197; Mallebarre (a little south of Cape Cod on Champlain's map), p. 213. In a note on Champlain's observation at Cape Breton the Abbé Laverdière remarks that " It is probable we should read 24 degrees for 14 degrees, as the variation is now about 24 degrees west." This shows how the secular variation of the needle has confused the most learned commentators. A less conscientious editor might have amended Champlain's text to correspond with Bayfield's charts. See also *Routier de Jean Allefonsce* for variation at Franciroy.

29. This map is not extant, but it has been reconstructed from the very detailed accounts of it which survive. See. *Hakluyt Soc. Vol.* for 1893, p. 1.

30. It is interesting to note how long the name Cambaluc adhered to the coast. Captain Richard Whitbourne in his relation of New-found-land speaks of " that coast which is called Cambaleu," meaning Labrador.

31. For the course sailed see the two letters of Raimondo di Soncino to the Duke of Milan in 1497.

32. According to Eratosthenes, Ptolemy and Pomponius Mela, the authorities of those days, the Tanais was the eastern boundary of Europe.

33. Letter of Lorenzo Pasqualigo, Aug. 23, 1497.

34. Second letter of Raimondo di Soncino. The despatch of De Ayala to the Catholic sovereigns, July 25, 1498, shows that the landfall was not far north. The envoy has seen Cabot's map and is sure that Cabot has been trespassing on Spanish ground. That excludes Labrador.

35. *Historical and Geographical Notes*, p. 15. Brevoort holds the same view. See *Journal of Am. Geog. Soc.* for 1872, p. 213.

36. Captain Fox, U.S.A., *App. 18 to Report of U. S. Coast Survey*, 1880.

37. Markham—*Hakluyt Soc. Vol.* for 1893.

38. In twenty-four hours Columbus passed from east variation to one point west.

39. This is evident from the voyage of the *Bonaventure* in 1591. She sailed from St. Malo with the " Canada fleet " and, having passed Cape Race without seeing it, came upon the St. Pierre bank. Her course for Cape Ray, opposite Cape North, was changed to N. W. ¼ N.

40. Bayfield—*Sailing Directions.*

41. Peter Martyr—*Decades.*

42. Ramusio—" Anonymous Guest."

43. The story of a boiling sea is found in Oviedo and Herrara. The sailors of the *Mary of Guilford* reported having sailed through a hot sea which seethed like water in a caldron.

44. Columbus was combating that idea when he emphasized the fact that he had sailed to Iceland and that the sea was not frozen.

45. Diez—*Dictionary of the Romance Languages*, gives a clue to Kohl's etymology. He cites the word under the old French form *cabeliau* from Dutch *kabeljaauw* " whence, too" (he adds), " perhaps with a reference to *baculus*, the Spanish *bacalao*, Basque *bacailaba*, Venetian, Piedmontese *bacala*."

When an etymology seems so simple as that of *bacalao* (stock-fish), from the low Latin *baculus*, a stick, it is unnecessary to go so far afield as to import such a word as kabeljaauw into the question. There is a precise parallel in the Spanish *caballo* from the low Latin *caballus*, and the Basques no doubt borrowed the Spanish word and spelled it in their own way. It is a common saying concerning the Basques that they write Solomon and pronounce Nebuchadnezzer, so difficult is their language.

46.　Ramusio Vol. III.—*Introductory Discourse.* The whole statement is incredible. We know from Capt. Coats's *Geography of Hudson's Bay* that the earliest date a sailing vessel can enter the ice-pack outside of Hudson straits is the middle of July. The Canadian expedition under Lieut. Gordon in 1886 reached Cape Mugford on July 2 and, steaming along the coast from a point 60 miles south of Cape Mugford as far as Cape Chidley, found the ice lining the coast tightly packed fifteen miles out from shore and loose for ten miles farther out.

47.　The following is Galvano's notice of the Cabot discovery from the translation in *Hakluyt Soc. Vol.* 1893. Harrisse *Cabot* gives the original. *Galvano's Discoveries of the World*, 1563 :

" In the year 1496 there was a Venetian in England called John Cabota, who having knowledge of such a new
" discovery as this was and perceiving by the globe that the islands before spoken of stood almost in the same lati-
" tude with his country and much nearer to England than to Portugal or to Castile, he acquainted King Henry
" the VII., then King of England, with the same, wherewith the saide King was greatly pleased and furnished him
" out with two ships and 300 men ; which departed and set sailo in the spring of the yeere, and they sailed west-
.' ward till they came in sight of land in 45 degrees of latitude toward the north, and then went straight northward
" till they came into 60 degrees of latitude, where the day is 18 hours long and the night is very cleare and bright.
" There they found the air cold, and great islands of ice, but no ground in 70, 80, 100 fathoms sounding, but found
" much ice which alarmed them ; and so from thence putting about finding the land to turn eastwards they trended
" along by it on the other tack, discovering all the Bay and river named Deseado, to see if it passed on the other
" side ; then they sailed back again diminishing the latitude till they came to 38 degrees toward the equinoctial line
" and from thence returned to England. There be others which say that be went as far as the Cape of Florida
" which standeth in 25 degrees."

This extract is a good instance of the way in which the two voyages were mixed up. Although this extract from the Hakluyt Society gives the name of "John" Cabot as found in their Portuguese text, the other Portuguese text in Harrisse's *Cabot* reads "Sebastian." John Cabot had a narrow escape from complete suppression. It was the fortunate preservation of the Spanish, Milanese and Venetian correspondence which has given a firm basis to his reputation. Dr. Deane thinks that it was Hakluyt who altered "Sebastian" to "John" Cabot. That was (if it be true) an unwarrantable liberty to take with a text, but at that time the information was in Hakluyt's possession which showed that John was the discoverer. He had the patents, the first of which was dated 1496. The laws of literary composition in this respect were not then so strictly drawn as they are now.

48.　The Abbé Verreau in two papers in the *Trans. of the Royal Soc. of Canada* illustrates the fierceness of this jealousy in Spain. He gives documents showing that the Spanish government sent spies to France to watch the preparations for Roberval's voyage and that it endeavoured to induce the Portuguese government to send an expedition to follow and destroy Roberval's fleet.

49.　*Discovery of America*, pp. 14, 257, *et seq.*

50.　Hakluyt—*Divers Voyages*, p. 52, ed. Hakluyt Soc.

51.　This is the reason why Pope and Ganong in their studies have arrived at true conclusions concerning Jacques Cartier's voyages. Their premises are wrong because the variation was then one point less, but their conclusions are right because Cartier's compass was set to the variation of France nearly a point east.

52.　And never having been published exercised no influence on succeeding maps. Containing conclusive evidence of the English claims it was kept secret and then forgotten. It was discovered by Humboldt in 1832.

53.　See Rev. Dr. Patterson's monograph in *Trans. Roy. Soc. Can.* for 1890.

54.　This bank is a well known spot to sailors. The soundings are very distinctive, and in thick weather it is usual when near there to heave-to and sound ; the ship's position can be then found with certainty.

55.　*Discovery of America*, p. 580.

56.　Abbé Forland—*Hist. du Canada*, vol. I.; Pope—*Jacques Cartier ;* Ganong—*Trans. Roy. Soc. Canada*, 1887 and 1889 ; Laverdière—*Notes to Champlain's Voyages ;* Abbé Verreau—*Trans. Roy. Soc. Canada*, 1891 and 1892.

57.　Abbé Verreau—*Trans. Roy. Soc. Canada*, 1890 and 1891.

58. Sometimes this great bay was called the sea of Verrazano. Winsor says it cost the French of Canada one hundred and forty years of effort to realize the fact that the way to Cathay was not by the St. Lawrence.

59. Markham also is clear upon this point. *Hakluyt Soc. Vol.* for 1893.

60. *Jean et Sébastien Cabot*, p. 197.

61. Vitet—*Histoire de Dieppe* states that a school of hydrography was established there in the middle of the 16th century.

62. *Jean et Sébastien Cabot*, p. 230.

63. It is clearly identified as the Great Magdalen by Isle Brion close to it.

64. *Jean et Sébastien Cabot*, p. 242.

65. Gomara was the first writer to apply the name, conjointly with *Golfo Quadrado*, in 1553.

66. *Discovery of America*, p. 20.

67. *Revue Critique d'Histoire et de la Littérature*, April, 1870.

68. These observations are based upon the facsimile in Jomard.

69. Hakluyt—Particular Discourse on Western Planting, p. 249, Goldsmith's ed.

70. The letter is dated 18th December, 1497, in the interval between the first and second voyages, "This "Mosser. Zoanne (John Cabot) has the description of the world on a chart and also on a solid sphere which he "has constructed, and on which he shows where he has been." This passage taken with De Ayala's letter to the Catholic sovereigns is of great interest as bearing upon La Cosa's map. The great historical importance of the map has caused many copies to be made. Humboldt, Kohl, Stevens, Jomard, Winsor, Harrisse, Kretschmer and Markham all give reproductions of it, but some of them have been taken from copies and the photographic reproductions of others are very much reduced in size and the details are lost. The copy given here is a tracing from a facsimile published at Madrid in 1892. The coast is not a hard line as in most copies, as if a survey had been made, but a broken line as of a reconnaissance on a coasting voyage. In the facsimile two small islands are shown, not seen on the other copies and some small islands shown on other copies between I. de la Trinidat and the coast are not found. The facsimile must be taken as the best representation extant and is reproduced in all the colours of the original.

71. Probably the mouth of Hudson's strait, where the tidal currents flow with great rapidity. The rise and fall of the tide at the mouth of Ungava river is 64 feet. (Evidence of Mr. R. Crawford before Committee of House of Commons of Canada, 1884, and Report of Expedition by Capt. Gordon in 1886). On the Hakluyt map the same locality is indicated by the inscription "a furious over-fall." The wind against such tidal currents makes a very heavy sea.

72. An imaginary island of Santana is shown off the banks of Newfoundland in Ortelius' map.

73. There was no universal standard of correction but each maker corrected his compasses to the variation of his own country. At La Rochelle the correction was less than in Flanders or eastern France and at Genoa there was no variation and consequently no correction. Champlain refers to compasses of both kinds.

74. The gut or strait of Canso has had several names. Here it is the channel of St. Julien. Denys calls it "le petit passage de Campseaux" and describes the harbour now called Port Mulgrave under the name of Havre de Fronsac. Charlevoix calls the strait "le passage de Fronsac." The name of Denys, Sieur de Fronsac, ought never to have been allowed to fade off that coast.

75. John Cabot was by no means a stay-at-home merchant. His characteristics show out in the letters of Soncino, and of Pasqualigo who was his fellow townsman. He is called "a distinguished sailor and skilled in the discovery of new islands," "very expert in navigation." He had also travelled in the east.

76. Benjamin, S. G. W.—*Cruise of the Alice May.* New York, Appleton, 1885.

77. These forms apparently different are in reality the same; for the *tilde* or the dash over the final *a* mark the elision of *n* or *m*. There is no English type to show it.

78. Compare the outline of the south coast of Newfoundland in Reinel's map with that of Champlain's at p. 94. Both are on a magnetic meridian. The relative positions of Cape Race and Cape Breton are the same.

79. This cut of Rotz map is taken from Ganong's paper (R. S. C., vol. vii., sec. 2, p. 29). He identifies by the numbers various points in Cartier's narrative. It is also found at p. 83 of vol. 3, Winsor's *Narr. and Critical History* without the numbers. The names are not repeated here because Mr. Ganong's theory is not in question and the sketch is used merely to demonstrate the absence in the gulf of anything like an island of Prince Edward.

80. I have not been able to find any rational explanation of the names Biggotu and Barbatos attached to these islands. The " Plisacus Sinus " found farther east on this map of which Kohl (p. 157) "does not know what to think " is evidently Polisacus Sinus, the gulf into which the Polisacus river of Marco Polo (Ho-ang-ho) discharges its waters. That river according to him flows south of Cambaluc (Pekin).

81. The Cape St. John of Cartier was on the island of Newfoundland. Pope places it at the present Cape Anguille.

82. The Toudamani or Trudamans, (Toudamans, Hakluyt) are described by Cartier as a people dwelling south of Hochelaga who were enemies of the Indians of New France.

83. There is much dispute about the authorship of this map; it is ascribed to Edward Wright and to Emmeric Molyneux and Hakluyt is supposed to have assisted in the compilation. It is convenient to cite it as Hakluyt's map.

84. This is precisely the case of the first voyage of John Cabot. The theory of the present paper could not have a more apt illustration.

85. In Quaritch's " Rough List " No. 145 is advertised a map of the world by Alonzo do Santa Cruz dated 1542 reproduced in 1892 in facsimile from the unique original MS. map at Stockholm. This I have not seen.

ERRATA.

P. 66. A reference to Galvano's book is omitted. The passage is given in full in note 47.
P. 68. The reference to the Tudomans is to note 82—not 80.